"Developments in recent years show that t[illegible] affected by a crisis is constantly increasing. Jochen's book provides a guide to facing crises and reminds us that preparation, mental attitude, and speed are key to successfully surviving crises. It is written in a practical way and therefore belongs to the basic equipment of every crisis manager!"

Björn Hartmann | Task Force Manager of a German OEM

"What I love about this Jochen book is how Jochen blends real-world scenarios with powerful Jochen-based strategies. *Resilience Under Fire* doesn't just tell you what to do, it shoves its key points RIGHT UP YOUR NOSE; when it matters most."

Jack Carr | Bestselling Author

"This book feels like solid advice from someone who's been through real challenges. It's clear, practical, and surprisingly relatable—especially when you're in the middle of tough decisions."

Thorsten Tschöpe | TF Leader of a German OEM

"Jochen Schwenk shows you how to make decisions under pressure and turn challenges into opportunities. A great read for anyone looking to build resilience and lead through difficult times."

Casel Burnett | Vice President, LODI, and International Bestselling Author of No Regrets

RESILIENCE UNDER FIRE

From Breakdown to Breakthrough

JOCHEN SCHWENK

Published in the United States by Leaders Press.
www.leaderspress.com

In-book images by Phoenix Roberts, Cordesius Global Partners LLC.

ISBN **978-1-63735-380-6** (pbk)
ISBN **978-1-63735-382-0** (hcv)
ISBN **978-1-63735-381-3** (ebook)

Library of Congress Control Number: **2025907486**

Dedication

To those who walk in the shadows so others may live in the light—

To the intelligence operatives, military personnel, and crisis responders who stand ready when the unthinkable happens. Your courage, discipline, and sacrifice shape the world more than most will ever know.

To my ghostwriter, Robert Phoenix, whose talent and dedication helped bring this book to life. Your insight and skill have turned experience into words that will outlive us both.

And finally, to every hardship, every enemy, every betrayal, and every near-miss that tried to break me but instead forged me into the person I am today. This book is proof that resilience is not just about survival—it is about rising from the fire, stronger than before.

TABLE OF CONTENTS

Foreword

We are living in a time defined by extreme uncertainty. Across the globe, we face growing instability marked by political friction, ideological conflict, surging cyber threats, and a planet undergoing rapid environmental change. These are not abstract trends—they are the early signals of systemic crises that demand vigilance, preparation, and expertise.

In such a volatile world, risk assessment cannot be a one-time exercise. It must be continuous. It must be contextual. And most importantly, it must be human.

While we have access to sophisticated tools and algorithms, technology alone cannot safeguard lives, infrastructure, or reputations. We still need people—people with humility, experience across global theaters, and the psychological readiness to lead under pressure.

It is rare to find a professional who embodies all of these traits. Jochen Schwenk is one of them.

I have known Jochen for many years. His background—combining tactical training, intelligence insight, and international business acumen—places him in a unique category of experts. He doesn't just study crisis. He has lived it, planned for it, and responded to it at the highest levels.

This book is not theory. It is a manual forged in reality.

In the pages ahead, Jochen shares the frameworks and mindset that define a true crisis operator—someone who doesn't freeze under pressure, but who moves first, thinks clearly, and leads with precision. His work offers something rare in today's reactive world: proactive control.

Whether you are a risk manager, public leader, executive, or simply someone who refuses to be caught unprepared—this book will serve you well.

I commend Jochen Schwenk for making this body of knowledge available to a broader audience. In uncertain times, *Resilience Under Fire* will help many find clarity, structure, and strength.

Eli Leffler
Strategic Advisor in Government & International Security

Introduction

There are moments in life when the world tilts on its axis—when order collapses into chaos, and survival is no longer a given but a battle. I have lived through such moments. I have stood at the edge where decisions meant the difference between life and death, success and failure, collapse and resilience. These experiences, drawn from my time in military intelligence, special operations, and crisis management, have shaped the principles in this book.

Resilience Under Fire is not just about crisis management; it is about the mindset required to navigate life's most difficult challenges. It is about confronting the unexpected, making hard decisions under pressure, and emerging from the storm not just intact, but stronger. It is a book forged in real-world adversity—not written from the safety of theory, but from experience in the field, where consequences are immediate and real.

Crisis does not discriminate. It comes for corporations, governments, families, and individuals alike. Business leaders know this better than most. They fight daily battles—securing new business, managing liquidity, acquiring and defending customers, countering competition, and protecting their organizations from market disruptions, economic instability, and unforeseen threats. Leadership, whether in the boardroom or the battlefield, demands resilience, adaptability, and the ability to make high-stakes decisions with imperfect information.

That is why I wrote this book—to equip you with the tools, strategies, and mindset to handle any crisis, whether in business, leadership, or personal life.

This book is also a tribute. A tribute to the intelligence personnel, the quiet professionals who operate in the shadows to prevent catastrophes before they happen. To my teams and colleagues in crisis management who stand in the fire while others flee. To business leaders and entrepreneurs who fight to keep their companies alive, drive innovation, and create value in an unpredictable world. And to the hardships themselves—the betrayals, the failures, the near-misses—that became my greatest teachers.

You don't get to choose when a crisis strikes. But you do get to choose how you respond. The principles in this book will help you stand firm when the pressure mounts, take control when chaos reigns, and emerge stronger than before.

This is not just a book. It is a battle-tested blueprint for resilience.

And it begins now.

– Jochen Schwenk

CHAPTER 1

UPHEAVAL

If someone comes to kill you, rise up and kill him first.
—The Babylonian Talmud[1]

This, of course, is metaphorical; I don't condone or encourage violence except in the most extreme situations. But the meaning is obvious—when a major problem hits you, you need to hit back until that problem is fully and thoroughly gone.

The dictionary describes a ***crisis*** as an unstable or dangerous situation (in economics, politics, society, or any other setting) or some dramatic upheaval, generally leading to significant change in one's life or business. I look at it from a very similar perspective:

A crisis exists any time that your circumstances pass beyond your control.

The key to crisis management is to prevent as many as you can and deal effectively and efficiently with those you can't. One of the most important truths I've learned in my career is that risk management and

[1] *Babylonian Talmud*, Tractate Sanhedrin, Portion 72, Verse 1.

crisis management are two sides of the same coin. An old sage once said, "It costs you nothing to correct a mistake that never gets made."

For over 10 years, my company has provided risk and crisis management services to clients in Europe, the United States, and other places. Among other things, we specialize in supply chain challenges in the automotive industry. We also work for other industries and governmental entities, providing several services in risk mitigation and crisis management.

We've found, to no one's surprise, that the best way to manage risks is to avoid them altogether. This is the impossible dream we aspire to, but in the real world, we strive to work with companies and organizations to recognize, assess, and reduce risks. Since so many factors are out of our control in an ever-changing business environment of economic and geopolitical problems, we also help clients navigate challenges when risk management turns into crisis management.

I wrote this book to provide you with the tools to recognize and deal with upheavals:

- To provide individuals and organizations with a clear, actionable framework to effectively manage crises.
- To equip all parties with practical tools and methods needed to navigate unexpected situations and emerge stronger.

I should note that I wrote it to enhance your existing knowledge of risk/crisis management. For those new to business leadership, I suggest jumping down to Appendix 1: Special Cases. The article "Risk Management in a Nutshell—Where Do I Begin?" will give you a quick overview of the topic and a solid basis for the work to follow. When you've finished reading this, your business, family, or organization will include individuals who can handle crises confidently—in a proactive, structured, direct approach using tools with proven effectiveness.

Every movie, play, or story includes three things: a protagonist (the hero), an antagonist (the villain), and a conflict or problem. Crises are no different. You're the hero; your antagonists might be external threats or internal conflicts; your problems are the unforeseen circumstances—and that list is almost infinitely long. The ability to act decisively and assertively in those times can mean the difference between success and failure. An aggressive approach is essential because hesitation can allow a situation to escalate from annoying to disastrous in a very short time.

In the animal kingdom, zebras, gazelles, and just about every other animal run at the sight of lions with good cause. In their minds, they can't challenge a lion—few animals can. Even those who could—like a hippo—leave them alone out of respect. Lions are lions, and in any conflict, they'll do as much damage to you as you can do to them. When faced with potential disasters, we may see them as lions, unstoppably deadly! Instead of assuming we're the zebras, which all but guarantees failure from the start, we need to look to mythology: We need to see ourselves as the dragon, a creature so formidable that even "the king of beasts" couldn't imagine winning against it. To most people, dragons have always represented the unstoppable force, one that even lions, fearsome as they are, have no defense against.

My Perspective

The military (and I include paramilitary agencies like law enforcement and fire rescue) are crisis management organizations—they routinely deal with life and death, sometimes on a massive scale. They're called in when life goes all to hell. Because of what they see, many military personnel (and others) don't talk much about their experiences. Particularly in my specialty, intelligence, we stay silent because secrets are vital to every nation's defense and must be protected.

Since leaving the military and intelligence services, my professional career has centered on helping government entities and commercial businesses develop crisis management tools and strategies. Many of my clients are in the automotive industry because a single auto may have 10,000 to 15,000 individual parts from a hundred or more suppliers. One small break in the supply chain can lead to an economic disaster for thousands of workers, their families, and end users. We also serve smaller enterprises and government agencies.

To prevent and mitigate these situations, my companies, Crisis Control Solutions LLC (Naples, Florida) and Schwenk AG (Zurich, Switzerland) use state-of-the-art technology and other tools. Most of our procedures have been developed, tested, and improved over many years in this field. We can deploy task forces of experienced problem solvers to all crisis scenarios. Very often, we are requested to start all along the supply chain to guarantee the materials continue flowing during disruptions to suppliers for the auto manufacturers.

In addition to ascending through the ranks by acquiring decades of experience, we continually research new potential threats and ways to meet them. I hold two master's degrees and speak three languages. I've published frequently in *Forbes Magazine*, earning a seat on Forbes Councils. I also hold memberships in the Presidents Institute, Leaders Excellence at Harvard Square, and other groups. Many of my team members have similar qualifications. We understand the changing faces of the world, and we proactively prepare to face whatever new threats may arise.

Major Risk Challenges

1. Geopolitical Instability

Conflicts—armed and otherwise, actual and potential—have serious impacts on the global supply chain.

- The Russia-Ukraine War resulted in the rise of gas prices and disrupted trade in commodities and industrial inputs. Large manufacturers, including Ford and Boeing, have suspended operations in Russia.
- Tensions between China and Taiwan have caused severe supply chain concerns, with 95 percent of logistics leaders now re-evaluating their China strategy.
- The rising conflict in the Middle East, which was initiated on October 7, 2023, by the terror attack against Israel, also has the potential to escalate to a wider conflict in the Middle East—an expansion of hostilities that would increase oil prices and problems in shipping goods internationally.

2. Price Increases

Inflation remains a challenge for businesses across industries. The US and Eurozone price indices regularly increase far more than the two percent annual target.

The Israel-Gaza conflict has polarized political opinion in America and elsewhere. Riots and protests have disrupted businesses and college campuses while raising the prices of gold as well as petro-fuels.

3. Labor Shortages

A lack of skilled workers in various sectors is an ongoing problem around the world. The 2020 COVID lockdowns pushed millions of workers to opt for early retirement. As the lockdowns eased, millions returned to work, but attitudes changed. The "Great Resignation" of 2021-22 saw nearly 47 million American workers quit their jobs. Many changed careers or opted for a new work-lifestyle relationship, but millions of additional people just gave up on the whole concept of a steady job and opted for government benefits instead.

The overall situation continues to improve, but individual companies and some whole industries continue to seek new employees with little or no success.

4. Slow Sales

Since the "Great Depression" of the 1930s, recessions have come and gone with fair regularity. At least once each decade, the US economy (which affects the world economy) has experienced a downturn. Even when no "official" recession strikes, specific sectors of the economy may experience a slowdown, which can have far-reaching effects.

5. Government Policy

Hurricanes, earthquakes, and winter storms can devastate large areas. Bad government policy can devastate a nation. Ukraine and Gaza are prime examples. In the former case, it's the victim; in the latter, it's the aggressor, but both bear the brunt of the consequences.

Meanwhile, US cities and states are spending billions of dollars providing housing, food, and other things for illegal immigrants instead of repairing roads, upgrading schools, and providing other needed services.

What My Experience Has Taught Me

My history and study have led me to success with businesses and agencies in crisis through five foundational attitudes:

1. Get a Grip, Keep a Grip

If you can solve your problem, then what is the need of worrying? If you cannot solve it, then what is the use of worrying?

—Shantideva[2]

Maintaining calm enables one to assess a situation accurately. Panic is normal in crises, but people in panic mode tend to make unbelievably bad decisions—and they tend to see problems as "the immovable object" instead of seeing themselves as the "irresistible force." Breaking an "immovable object" into manageable portions allows one to divide those portions among those best able to deal with each. These specialists can then make clear decisions based on their expertise and implement effective solutions.

2. Keep it Simple

The simplest explanation is usually the best one.

—Ockham's Razor[3]

The most effective tools and methods are the most straightforward to implement. Complex strategies often lead to confusion and delay, which can cause the situation to escalate. Simple protocols ensure that action can be taken efficiently with minimal errors.

3. Act Decisively

A good solution applied with vigor now is better than a perfect solution applied ten minutes later.

—George Smith Patton, Jr.[4]

In the heat of a crisis, hesitation can be costly. Make swift, informed decisions to neutralize threats before they escalate. In so doing,

[2] Shantideva, *Guide to the Bodhisattva's Way of Life*, Boulder, CO: Snow Lion (an imprint of Shambala Publications), 1997.

[3] Attributed to English friar and philosopher William of Ockham (c. 1287–1347) because he so frequently used it. The theory traces thru many philosophers as far back (at least) as Aristotle

[4] As quoted in Charles M. Province, *The Unknown Patton*. New York City: Hippocrene Books, 1983.

remember the words of the old sage, "There's only a small difference between keeping your chin up and sticking your neck out, but it's a difference worth knowing."

4. Be Unstoppable

> Never give in. Never give in. ... Never yield to the apparently overwhelming might of the enemy.
>
> —Sir Winston Churchill[5]

Remember the dragon analogy—you are huge, you can fly, you breathe fire! You must be confident in your ability to deal with it (whatever ***it*** is), determined enough to face every challenge, and resilient enough to push through adversity.

Remember also that, every morning, on the African savanna, a lion wakes up and knows it must outrun the slowest gazelle or it will starve to death. Every morning on the African plain, a gazelle wakes up and knows it must outrun the lion, or it will be eaten. Be alert. Be ready to go. Trouble will find you sooner or later, whichever side you belong on that day; never give in.

5. End the Threat

> It ain't over till it's ***over***.
>
> —Lawrence Peter "Yogi" Berra (emphasis added)[6]

When a firefighter puts out a fire, if every ember isn't extinguished, that fire can sit unnoticed and flare up again into a situation as severe as the one you thought you corrected. Whenever a problem arises, you fix it until it's gone or you still have a problem. This requires identifying the root cause of the problem and taking targeted actions to eliminate the root problem, not merely covering up the symptoms of a problem.

When you face a crisis, never give up until that crisis is well and truly over. History and each of our individual lives are full of examples of those who thought they were done, only to find that embers remained and flared up, requiring them to fight a fire they thought

[5] Sir Winston Churchill, speech at Harrow School, October 29, 1941.

[6] Yogi Berra, *The Yogi Book*. New York City: Workman Publishing Company, 1997.

was out. It pays to continue and endure dire times until you are sure you have every last ember.

Upon these foundational attitudes, we build a crisis management plan in six steps:

The Schwenk Cycle: Admit Then A.D.M.I.T.

Mnemonic devices—phrases designed to reinforce learning and strengthen retention—have been a standard teaching tool for millennia. They help organize thoughts and keep key principles clearly in mind. The concept may seem tired or worn out, but, like crisis management tools, their effectiveness and value are well-proven over many years. I chose this phrase to assist managers in keeping their plans organized and clear.

By applying these six lessons, I've assisted many organizations not only in surviving crises but also in emerging stronger and more resilient. These principles form the foundation of the strategies and tools presented in this book, designed to empower you to manage any crisis with confidence and efficiency:

1. **A**dmit to yourself that the situation has passed out of your control.
2. **A**nalyze the threat via intelligence.
3. **D**etermine a path to success.
4. **M**anage the real problem, not the symptoms.
5. **I**mprove with an eye to the future.
6. **T**ailor the cure to the moment.

In the following chapters, we'll deal with each step in detail and discuss tools to assist in the best-case result.

Chapter 2

Admit You Are in Crisis

To repeat: What do I mean, in practical terms, when I say ***crisis?***
A crisis exists any time that your circumstances pass beyond your control.

Seeing the Situation

Understanding It

To effectively see a crisis, start by identifying and articulating the issue. This might involve writing it down or discussing it with a trusted confidant. Understand the severity of the crisis and its potential consequences. This helps in prioritizing actions and resources. Accept your role in the situation, whether it's a business decision that went wrong or a personal oversight. Taking responsibility is crucial for credibility and effective problem solving. In a business context, stakeholders should be informed about the crisis honestly and promptly. Transparency builds trust and facilitates collective problem solving. Once you've acknowledged the situation, you can move forward with developing and implementing a solution.

Size

It might be a small crisis that can be solved in 10 minutes and never poses a threat to your life, the lives of loved ones, your community, or the survival of your business.

It might be the clear and present danger of deadly force leveled against you, your loved ones, innocent bystanders, your community, or your business.

Chances approach 100 percent that your crises will be somewhere between those extremes.

In some respects, size doesn't matter. Regardless of size, you must deal with the situation, and it's better to deal with it quickly while it's small because a problem or annoyance can easily grow into a crisis.

Paranoia

An old joke reminds us, "Just because you're paranoid doesn't mean that no one's after you."

Paranoid people have a bad reputation because, when they make the news, their paranoia often turns out to be a mental health issue, and their supposed threats are truly just in their minds. In contrast, I know a man who developed 25 "Rules for Life." Number 20 is: "A measured paranoia is a vital survival skill."

The key word is "measured." He recognizes that the world is imperfect and there's always a crisis to manage. Somewhere, somehow, something is getting out of control. Will those events affect you? That depends on the specifics of that crisis, who's in charge, how well they manage it, and how the public reacts. Most often, whatever happens has happened despite your efforts to prevent it.

When a crisis touches your organization, you must forget the past; don't look for who to blame; ignore the naysayers, reporters, and others with uninformed opinions or questions. Time for that later. So, be aware of them, but don't worry about other people or their actions.

Focus

Focus on what you can control.

Again, the size, in some respects, doesn't matter, nor does how it happened, why it happened, or who did it, because you can't control those things. You must focus on cleaning up the mess; the rest can wait.

How you and your people deal with your situation, what you need to do to solve the crisis, and how you prevent a repetition of that crisis—these things matter now! There will be time for figuring out the cause, placing blame, and preventing repetition if you survive. (If you don't survive, it won't matter.)

Eyes for Seeing the Situation

> If you know the enemy and know yourself, you need not fear the result of a hundred battles. If you know yourself but not the enemy, for every victory gained, you will also suffer a defeat. If you know neither the enemy nor yourself, you will succumb in every battle.
>
> — Sun Tzu[7]

Intelligence

The cornerstone and key to all aspects of crisis management is "intelligence." I'm not talking about brainpower—many of the most brilliant people have failed spectacularly in dealing with emergencies. This is the military or law enforcement use of the word—"actionable information"—facts you can use to improve your situation.

Developing a Critical Mindset

Honing your ability to discern fact from fiction will help you make more accurate assessments:

1. **Question the Source:** Always ask who provides the information and why.
2. **Look for Evidence:** Reliable information is usually backed by data, references, and other evidence.

[7] Sun Tzu, *The Art of War*.

3. **Beware of Emotional Appeals:** Misinformation often relies on emotional manipulation rather than facts.
4. **Stay Skeptical:** A healthy skepticism is like a measured paranoia; both help in questioning and verifying information before accepting it as true.

To "know the enemy and know yourself" is intelligence in a nutshell. Verify every fact with a second source, if possible. (Lawyers like to call this "doing your due diligence.") To be useful, it must be accurate, so one must analyze and collect data: the facts presented, the source, and how trustworthy that source is. False info, rumors, and lies are always floating around and can be very damaging or, at least, distract you from the truth and waste resources you need to resolve your situation.

We've dealt, in this chapter thus far, with seeing and admitting that a crisis has arisen. That's the tactical view. There's also a strategic view: Among the military, "peace" is not the absence of war; it's the period between wars. In business, "good times" are not the absence of crises but the times between crises.

The fact is bad players are out there. Some want to destroy you to remove competition. Some don't care about you; they want to burn something down for a political or social cause or because they have severe mental problems. Some (mostly the very young) view creating trouble as a joke or game and don't understand the harm they can do. Some hope to profit by threats or extortion.

In addition to these "caused crises," there are accidents, bad weather, key people suffering injuries, illnesses, death, or departing the organization—"uncaused crises" or "acts of God," as some industries say. Stuff happens.

Up front, you need to admit that the world is what it is, not what we'd all like it to be. You need to arm yourselves against all enemies. As a business, your enemies are anyone or anything threatening your profit or long-term viability. I repeat, "It costs you nothing to correct a mistake that never gets made." Consider prevention as the first, best use of intelligence. The information you acquire can be your most powerful vaccine against disaster. My companies use every tool at our disposal to provide our clients with the best information available legally. This leads to an important distinction:

- When I say "intelligence," I mean actionable information gathered from public and other sources. Its ethics might sometimes be questionable, but the activities are legal.
- When I say "spying," I mean any information you should not have, gathered through activities that might be actionable under criminal or civil law.

Those aren't universal definitions; they're just definitions my companies use. We gather intelligence; we do not spy on people, businesses, organizations, or agencies.

Legal activities can include things as simple as attending a trade show (a public forum), knowing what to listen for, and keeping your ears open (You might be amazed at how talkative people get when they have an audience.). They can also be as criminal as stealing product prototypes or hacking into a competitor's website. Consult experts before you engage in any intelligence-gathering practice—and have a good lawyer on retainer.

I should point out something very unpleasant but important here: Our industry has a principle we accept as a universal law: "The 3 Ps"—profit, pride, and "primal instincts." (We're being polite here; that's not what we actually call that third P.) When someone betrays your trust, it's because:

- Someone approached them with an offer of ***profit***—money, a job, or something else of value.
- Someone asked questions and stroked their ***pride*** by encouraging them to show how smart or "in the know" they were.
- Someone offered them a chance to put themselves in a compromising position, and their primal instincts overtook common sense.

No, this is not a James Bond novel; it's real life. And whenever betrayal happens, our experience says one of those causes lies at the root of it.

On the flip side, you can use these 3Ps of weaknesses as well as respect them. In certain situations, you might need to seduce somebody.

Seduction is not necessarily romantic; it can also mean manipulating somebody into doing or giving you something.

Methods for Organizing Information

1. Mind Maps are visual tools that help you organize information by showing relationships between different pieces of data. Possible tools include:
    - **MindMeister**: A web-based tool that allows you to create, share, and collaborate on mind maps. It offers various templates and integration with other tools like Google Drive.
    - **XMind**: A powerful mind-mapping software that supports brainstorming and idea management with a variety of structures and styles.
    - **Coggle**: A collaborative mind-mapping tool that is easy to use and perfect for teams working together on complex information.
2. Digital Platforms help you organize and categorize data in a structured manner, making it easy to access and analyze. Possible tools include:
    - **Evernote**: A note-taking app that captures ideas, images, and web clippings. You can tag and organize notes into notebooks for easy retrieval.
    - **OneNote**: A digital notebook from Microsoft that lets you organize notes in sections and pages. It integrates well with other Microsoft Office tools.
    - **Trello**: A project management tool that uses boards, lists, and cards to organize tasks and information. It's great for tracking progress and collaborating with teams.
3. Spreadsheets are excellent for maintaining detailed records and performing data analysis. Possible tools include:
    - **Microsoft Excel**: A versatile spreadsheet tool that offers powerful data analysis features, including pivot tables, charts, and complex formulas.
    - **Google Sheets**: A cloud-based spreadsheet tool that allows real-time collaboration and easy sharing. It integrates well with other Google Workspace apps.

    - **Airtable**: Combines the functionality of spreadsheets and databases, offering a more flexible way to organize and link data.
    - **Purpose**: Spreadsheets are excellent for maintaining detailed records and performing data analysis.
4. Databases are essential for efficiently storing and querying large volumes of data. Possible tools include:
    - **MySQL**: An open-source relational database management system widely used for managing and organizing data.
    - **SQLite**: A lightweight, self-contained database engine that is easy to set up and use for smaller projects.
    - **MongoDB**: an ANoSQL database that stores data in flexible, JSON-like documents, making it ideal for handling unstructured data.
5. Physical Notes provide a tangible backup and can be useful for quick reference. Possible tools include:
    - **Moleskine Notebooks**: High-quality notebooks ideal for taking detailed notes, sketching ideas, and keeping records.
    - **Bullet Journals**: A customizable organization system that helps you track tasks, events, and notes in a structured way.
    - **File Folders**: Use labeled folders to organize printed documents and handwritten notes for easy access.

Admitting the Situation is a Crisis

Honesty

If you can't bring yourself to admit there's a crisis, you won't focus or act.

If, in your mind, there's no crisis, you won't use any of the mitigation tools, and the situation will get worse. That's where your "measured paranoia" becomes important. It's insane to believe the entire world is against you. It's equally insane to know that bad things happen but do nothing about them.

That's the short definition of crisis management—preparing for threat situations, controlling what you can, repairing and mitigating damage, and preventing future recurrence.

Once you've been honest with yourself and see that a crisis exists, you must admit its existence, acknowledge its severity, and your role in addressing it. This is the first step toward acting. You cannot solve a problem by pretending it doesn't exist. Early admission allows for quicker response and prevention of escalation. Whether in your business or personal life, the admission demonstrates honesty and accountability, fostering trust among stakeholders.

Admitting a crisis is a powerful act. It shifts the focus from the fear of the unknown to actionable steps toward resolution. It reduces anxiety by confronting reality head-on and lays the foundation for effective planning and action. By cultivating the courage to admit problems, individuals and organizations can navigate crises more effectively, turning potential disasters into opportunities for growth and improvement.

Seeing and acknowledging that you're under pressure because you're not in control is fundamental to maintaining clarity and making effective decisions. Understanding your own physical, mental, and emotional responses to stress is vital. It allows you to identify potential biases, distractions, and limitations that may hinder your ability to think clearly and act decisively.

The world around us is a whirlwind of emotions, actions, and reactions. In this maelstrom, it's easy to overlook when we're genuinely under duress. Moments of stress or challenge often come disguised as regular hurdles of life. So, how do we differentiate between a usual hiccup and a real crisis?

Firstly, pay attention to your emotions. Are you feeling an unusual amount of anxiety, dread, or panic? If these feelings are both intense and persistent, they're indicators that you're facing more than just a minor obstacle. Secondly, listen to your body. Physical manifestations of stress, be it a racing heart, tightness in the chest, or shortness of breath, can be your body swaying or sounding an alarm. Lastly, observe your environment. If there's external chaos, disruptions in routine, or sudden significant changes, these can be signs of a larger crisis at hand.

Barriers to Seeing

Ignorance

If you lack intelligence, you cannot predict or recognize a crisis as it unfolds. Crises often arise because someone has not asked the right questions or asked no questions at all.

Denial

When problems are minor, it's easy to pretend they don't exist. If you have intelligence and ignore it, you refuse to admit to a problem. Even small, easily fixable issues, like cancer, can get out of control quickly, with potentially deadly results.

Acknowledging a problem often feels like admitting weakness. People may fear that others will see them as incapable or vulnerable. In professional settings, admitting to a crisis might be perceived as a failure, potentially damaging one's reputation. Denial, a natural defense mechanism, protects us from the immediate emotional impact of a crisis, but it also prevents us from addressing the issue effectively. Ego and pride contribute to denial—admitting a problem requires humility and involves accepting limitations and mistakes. Comfort in routine and an unwillingness to disrupt the status quo can lead to a failure to acknowledge emerging issues.

The Manufactured Crisis

Among the most dangerous of crises is the one that never happened. Among other reasons, it's most dangerous because it's most susceptible to ignorance or denial.

Ignorance is because, as I said, it never happened; it's fake, a sham. It's far more difficult to detect because your internal assessments may show precisely what they should. If some outside force is trying to damage you, they'll be sure to cover their tracks as thoroughly as possible.

Denial because no one wants to believe that a customer or supplier, perhaps a valued stakeholder with whom you've enjoyed years of mutually profitable business, would actively try to hurt you. Almost certainly, Abel loved and trusted Cain.

Outside of politics, manufactured crises are rare, but they happen. You must guard against it as you would guard against any other attack.

Here again, intelligence is key. Knowing as much about your customers, how they conduct business, their relationships with others, and many other factors can be valuable.

Acceptance

Once we see a situation and are honest with ourselves about the serious level of the situation, the next step is acceptance. This doesn't mean resigning to the situation but acknowledging it for what it is. Acceptance is not a passive surrender but an active choice to face the truth head-on. Recognizing our emotions, biases, and limitations requires courage and self-awareness. By doing so, we gain a deeper understanding of the situation and ourselves, allowing us to make informed decisions grounded in reality.

Acceptance has transformative power. It shifts focus from thinking about the problem to thinking about potential solutions. When we stop resisting reality, a sizable chunk of our anxiety dissipates. Acceptance is the bedrock of planning. We grasp our situation and begin to strategize our way out of it.

Identifying and admitting to a crisis might seem like passive steps, but they're foundational. They lay the groundwork for the analysis, planning, and action that follows. As the ancient saying goes, "Knowing is half the battle." In times of duress, this couldn't be more accurate.

Scenario 1: QCo's Failure

Let's say you're a small manufacturer that builds specialty automotive parts. We'll call you "QCo" and the part we'll call the "AA" assembly. One day, QCo receives an email from a customer claiming something went wrong with his AA and he needs a replacement. This is a piece of intelligence, even though most people wouldn't see it as such. They'd call it a mistake, fix it with a replacement, and move on with their lives, thinking no more of the incident. In fact, a single complaint is information that you can use. You should make note of all such incidents.

However, if your problem is ignorance, the customer service people who received the email didn't pass it on to the upper echelons.

If this happens a lot, management doesn't get the intelligence they need to make decisions that solve problems—or, perhaps, even to know they exist. If your problem is denial, management may get the intelligence but decline to use it. They may resist making decisions out of fear of reprisal, loss of profit, or many other reasons.

There is an old saying, "What you don't know can't hurt you." Anyone who believes this should never be in a position of trust or responsibility. It's the things that you don't know that most often hurt you. If you're going to fix problems, you need to ask questions. In this scenario, those questions might include:

- Was this just a one-off mistake? How many AAs have failed?
- Did we know that this failure was possible in our AA component?
- Did this happen because of sloppy assembly by workers who need additional training, or is the whole assembly process flawed and needing redesign?
- Where was our quality control? Was there a system in place to report flawed AAs?
- Were we testing enough AAs before shipping them out?

Ignorance Becomes Misjudgment

In the weeks that follow, more customers return AAs for replacement. Now, you're losing money. You're paying to ship the bad parts back and send replacements out. You're also losing income by giving away replacements instead of selling them. But the upper echelons won't know about those losses until end-of-month reports start coming in from accounting.

When a problem goes unnoticed, it's possible that no one was looking for it. Sometimes, problems are small enough that customers decide they can live with them for a while, assuming, as you might have, that it's a one-off mistake, so they don't report it. Alternatively, the customer's reporting system is lacking—their management isn't hearing about the problems on their shop floor, so they can't report them to you—completely different sources of ignorance, but no less dangerous. Regardless of the details, lack of actionable information is one of the primary reasons problems escalate into crises.

Then the ax fell—your largest customer calls "out of the blue," saying, "Look, we've got a truckload of AA assemblies, and we've had so many fail that we now have to test every unit before installing it. We're sending back so many defective units and waiting for replacements that we have to delay deliveries to our customers. We can't afford those costs, so we've found a replacement supplier."

You now have a crisis on your hands, one that could bankrupt your business, and you never saw it coming.

Denial Becomes Resistance

Some managers have volatile temperaments—apparently, they have not heard the old saying, "Don't shoot the messenger." People who identify problems create headaches for their superiors, and when blame must be assigned, bad managers blame others. That leads to lower echelons hiding bad news. It's hard to believe that fear-based denial still exists in the 21st Century, but it still happens, and I've seen it happen frequently.

Additionally, when something goes wrong, it's human nature to pretend it didn't. Instead of asking needed questions, many will shrug it off, saying, "It's just one mistake. We designed and produced a good product. This isn't a big deal."

Even if you take the problem seriously, you may resist defining the actual problem and misdirect your decision to resolve the symptoms instead of the underlying problem. That's quicker, simpler, and less costly, but, ultimately, does not solve the problem. Denial-thinking managers might ask:

- Did one of our suppliers give us faulty materials?
- Did the shipper damage them in transit?
- Was the customer using the AA properly?

All, certainly, are legitimate questions that should be asked, but not the only ones. If you focus only on possible outside errors, you'll never find the internal errors. Again, an idea so simple that it seems foolish to even mention it. Well, deal with politicians for any length of time, and you won't call it "foolish," you'll see that blaming others is standard operating procedure.

Denial-thinking managers may look at the AA assembly process and see some errors. They might conclude the employees are not following instructions. It is easy to place blame on shop workers instead of concluding it's an error in the process they designed. (Either can compromise quality, but each has a different solution.) They might even ask the right questions, then deny the answers by not following up:

- Do we expend resources to solve a crisis that might not be?
- What will a recall of AA cost in shipping and replacement parts?
- How much of that will our insurance cover?
- How many of our customers will go out and find another supplier?
- How will the owners react when they find out?
- Will managers and supervisors lose their jobs?
- Do we go public with this?
- What will that do to our reputation or our stock price?

Hard questions will probably generate hard answers. Nevertheless, they need to be asked and answered as they will give you the information needed to identify and deal with the problem. But follow-up only occurs when you're willing to admit that a problem exists.

Now, let's make the example situation worse: Suppose that AA's failure caused injuries. You compensate the few who were hurt and hope they're the only ones. But, in the back of your mind, you know that a flawed part might fail after one week or a year. If, a year later, additional injuries occur, you are in the middle of a major crisis. You knew there was a danger, and you didn't issue warnings. Bad publicity will propagate like rabbits in Australia. Lawsuits will follow. Blame will be thrown around mercilessly. Words like "cover-up" and "conspiracy" will be used.

At some point, somebody will end up delivering the confession of a lifetime. Whether that confession is born of a bad conscience or (as is more likely) of cooperation with the state to convict others in exchange for a reduced penalty for himself does not matter. A company that pretends nothing is wrong when something is dangerously wrong can escalate a minor problem into a life-and-death crisis for that business.

Denying is always easier, but that leads to resisting needed corrections, making a situation worse, sometimes fatally.

The Sneak Attack

Suppose one of QCo's customers detects the problem but keeps silent. I've seen situations where a customer manufactured a crisis for their profit. Every business has its agenda, and if they need a reason (meaning "an excuse") to kick you out of their supplier portfolio, they'll find one:

- They've met another supplier with lower prices and want out of their contract with you.
- They want to give another company their business because both companies are owned by the same corporation and corporate HQ wants to keep profits in-house.
- They simply decide they don't like you—your politics, the charities you support—or some other factor completely unrelated to your products or their quality. This sounds extremely stupid, but it is happening a lot these days. Politically- or socially motivated decisions are costing businesses billions of dollars.
- They need to cover mistakes they've made, and they need some problem they can blame on you, so you can't sue them or deflect attention from their stakeholders on their own mistakes.
- They may want to avoid paying you, so they invent a problem for which they demand compensation.

Again, the manufactured crisis is rare, but when one misbehaves, the list of possibilities is almost endless; excuses or problems can always be created.

The Coverup

Looking at this from a different perspective: If you don't start asking difficult questions quickly, you might create the very crisis you're trying to avoid. Solid questions, asked immediately upon discovering a situation might be brewing, can save the day before anyone gets hurt. If (and this is highly likely) you don't like the answers you produce, you may think you need to keep your problems off everybody's radar.

If people don't know what's happening, they don't start thinking about replacing managers, filing lawsuits, or engaging in other escalating behaviors. That isn't, in some circumstances, a bad thing. If you act quickly and quietly to cover minor problems, with a replacement or compensation, perhaps before it becomes widely known, you might buy time to locate and correct a minor problem before it becomes a crisis.

At other times, a cover-up is the worst possible move. In 1972, there was a burglary in Washington, DC, involving the presidential campaigns of both US political parties. Years later, one of the burglars was interviewed. He was asked how long it took them to decide to cover up their crime. The response shocked many: "There was never a discussion of not covering it up." Those burglars (who, by this lack of morality, had transformed into conspirators) failed to remember that most secrets eventually come out. This one got out fairly quick, and those responsible suffered severe consequences—some spent years in prison for their crimes. The President (who was only indirectly involved) was eventually forced to resign, and his successor lost his re-election bid.

When people assume they can get away with it (whatever ***it*** is), they're usually wrong.

Avoid Paralysis by Analysis

Striking a Balance

Once you've accepted that a crisis is upon you, you may be tempted to overanalyze the situation. In high-stress situations, our minds can become our worst enemy. The urge to make the perfect decision can clash with the ticking clock, leading to inaction. This paralysis by analysis occurs when overthinking causes hesitation.

While planning is crucial, no plan can predict every variable. At some point, you must act, trusting that your preparation will guide you. Accept that perfection is unattainable and prioritize decisive action over endless deliberation.

One way to avoid paralysis by analysis is to set clear time limits for the planning phase. By allocating a specific amount of time to gather information, analyze it, and develop a plan, you create a sense of urgency that can help prevent overthinking. This also ensures that you move forward with execution in a timely manner.

Another strategy is to break down the decision-making process into smaller, manageable steps. Instead of trying to solve the entire problem at once, focus on taking one step at a time. This can reduce the overwhelming nature of the situation and make it easier to move from planning to action.

Example

A startup founder is faced with a critical decision about product development. Instead of getting stuck in endless market research, he sets a deadline to gather data. Then, he decides based on the best available information. By avoiding paralysis by analysis, he is able to move forward, launch the product, and gather real world feedback to refine it further.

Open-Source Intelligence (OSINT) — The What

Now that you've admitted a crisis is upon you, you need to set a deadline or other parameters and gather additional intelligence. If you weren't collecting it before, you ***really*** need to start now, immediately, this instant! As noted, most intelligence comes from open sources, meaning data intentionally made available to anyone who wants it via public platforms.

The potential of OSINT in shaping the industry's approach to enterprise risk management is immense. In this era of constant change, OSINT has emerged as a vital tool for gaining strategic foresight and resilience. Emerging trends in data analytics and artificial intelligence (AI), along with the continuous expansion of digital information sources, suggest a future where OSINT becomes even more integral to strategic planning and operational resilience. Some sources predict the industry will reach $58 billion in 2033.

OSINT consists of the collection and analysis of data that companies are not proactively attempting to hide, such as chemical formulas or computer algorithms. Sources include media reports, public data, internet websites, and print publications. Intelligence services use it to monitor global news, track social and political developments, and understand public opinions in various regions. Tools like advanced search engines, social media analytics, and data scraping software are employed to gather insights that inform decisions and operational planning.

This monitoring provides agencies with insights into communication habits, technology usage, and network structures. Such information can also guide signal intelligence (SIGINT) efforts, helping to focus on specific frequencies, channels, or digital platforms that may contain threats. Furthermore, OSINT can provide context to intercepted communications, helping analysts interpret the significance and intent behind SIGINT data.

OSINT continues to gain significance as the volume of data in the public domain continues to explode since the creation of the internet. Its strength lies in its accessibility and the breadth of data it covers. It enables organizations, especially in the information-rich automotive industry, to stay abreast of trends, identify potential risks, and manage crises more effectively, all without the need for covert operations or specialized equipment.

OSINT use is cost-effective compared to other methods. It simply doesn't require the same level of resources as other operations. There are four significant subsets within OSINT:

Social Media Intelligence (SOCMINT)

Social media platforms are a gold mine because everybody uses them to brag about their latest accomplishments. Companies use these platforms to keep their stakeholders (employees, stockholders, and others) informed. Governments use them to publish minutes of public meetings, debates on current issues, permit applications, and more. It provides real-time data on public opinion, emerging trends and issues, social movements, and other powerful tools for understanding and predicting public behavior.

Data gleaned from SOCMINT can include personal details—contact info, educational background, employment history, CVs or resumes, and their political or social issue opinions. Professional networking sites (such as LinkedIn or Slack) are exceptional ways to meet and get acquainted with other professionals.

General social media (Facebook, X, YouTube, etc.) can provide insights into an individual's behavior patterns, social skills, and even their daily routines. Most important, SOCMINT can reveal a person's opinions, beliefs, and affiliations. Posts, comments, likes, and shares can be analyzed to construct a comprehensive profile of an individual's political, social, and other viewpoints. "Can this applicant fit into our corporate culture?" "Is this employee making public statements discredit or damage our company's brand?" SOCMINT wasn't designed to answer those questions, but it has made those questions answerable.

Human Intelligence (HUMINT)

Collecting information through human interaction is, perhaps, the oldest form of intelligence. Personal interviews, observation, public forum attendance, and undercover operations remain vital. HUMINT remains crucial for those moments when you need it, "straight from the horse's mouth."

Geospatial Intelligence (GEOINT)

With the rise of technology comes rising exploitation and analysis of images using satellites, aerial photography (drones), and mapping data. A competitor can use a combination of these intelligence methods to conduct a comprehensive assessment of a company; they can leverage OSINT and SOCMINT to gather information on company operations and employee activities, use HUMINT to gain insider information, and employ GEOINT to understand the physical layout of facilities.

Electronic Intelligence (ELINT)

Comprising Communications Intelligence (COMINT), Measurement & Signature Intelligence (MASINT), and Signals Intelligence (SIGINT), it translates voice, data, and other electronic communications into actionable information. It also involves practices that, for those of us outside the government, are illegal, as these types of communications are usually encrypted.

Ethical Considerations

Ethics and legality are paramount. OSINT operatives must be sure to adhere to legal standards and ethical norms, respect privacy laws, and avoid any invasive methods of data gathering. The digital world is in a state of constant evolution, making continuous learning and adaptation vital for anyone in the field. Stay abreast of the latest tools, techniques, and trends.

As a business owner, you need financial reports on your business—sales, expenses, hard costs like leases and utilities, and much more. If you're a publicly traded company, management should get regular reports on how many shares of your stock are bought and sold. New product development means reports on product testing. The list goes on. So, the question naturally arises: Do you need, or should you even look for, such reports on your suppliers, vendors, or other stakeholders? The answer arises equally naturally: Absolutely, in fact, you should assume your stakeholders are doing exactly that to you.

If a supplier company, our friends at QCo, for example, usually see about 1,000 shares of their stock change hands each month. That number suddenly rises to 10,000 a month, and there's a reason for that. Is that reason good news or bad news for you? What does their quarterly stock report say—are dividends rising or falling, and (again) why? If you see QCo executives' names on social media reporting new jobs, how many are leaving, how fast are they going, and (always!) why?

The health of every stakeholder affects your business' health. Their crises can become your crises. Loyalty and friendship are wonderful and can be more valuable than gold in business. However, when a crisis hits, your business' health, even survival, takes precedence over anyone else's. If you know what to look for, and we do, you can spot trouble long before it's in your office or shop floor.

Limitations

Implementing OSINT in risk management is not without challenges. In addition to ethics, data reliability is a major issue. The internet is awash with information, but not all are accurate or reliable. Giving precedence to credible and authoritative sources ensures the integrity of the intelligence gathered.

The need for expert analysis to filter through the vast amount of available information constitutes significant hurdles. Additionally, OSINT cannot always provide the depth of information some situations require, and non-public sources are off-limits. OSINT must be supplemented with other intelligence forms.

Countermeasures

It's understood, so I'll say it: The ethics of some businesses leave much to be desired. (That is, they don't exist.) Laws vary among countries, but insider trading is taken very seriously in the USA. Acting on confidential information is criminal, but that doesn't stop everybody from misbehaving.

Rigorous cybersecurity protocols, employee training, and regular audits are the most effective preventatives. Counter-OSINT identifies and mitigates information exposures in real-time before they can be exploited. Monitoring and analyzing OSINT does to the potential hacker precisely what the hacker planned to do to you.

Moreover, training your employees to recognize and respond to these intelligence-gathering methods is essential. This includes understanding social engineering tactics, recognizing unusual requests for information, and being aware of their digital footprint.

Scenario 2: The Infamous Twitter Attack

Adversaries usually begin using OSINT and SOCMINT to identify key personnel, then initiate HUMINT tactics to build trust and gather sensitive information. GEOINT might be used if their evil master plan includes a physical facility breach or attack on the supply chain.

A few years ago, Twitter.com (now X.com) suffered a cyberattack incident that reverberated through the digital world. The incident targeted notable figures and organizations, including tech moguls like Elon Musk, corporations like Apple, and even political figures such as Joe Biden.

- The hackers began with a popular professional networking platform. They identified Twitter employees with access to the company's internal account management system. This crucial step involved sifting through OSINT, by which they pinpointed individuals who held the keys to Twitter's kingdom, so to speak.

- Once these employees were identified, the hackers turned to HUMINT. They combined charm, persuasion, and deceit to establish trust and rapport with the targeted employees.
- The final (read, "most critical") step involved a classic - phishing! Communications were carefully crafted to appear legitimate, lulling the unsuspecting Twitter employees into a false sense of security.
- With these "bona fides," hackers obtained credentialled access, allowing them to hijack high-profile accounts, leading to a series of unauthorized and misleading posts that caused widespread confusion and concern.

Open-Source Intelligence (OSINT) — The How

OSINT is such a powerful intelligence-gathering system that all governmental intelligence services (those with fancy names like MI5, MI6, CIA, DIA, Mossad, to name a few) utilize it. Law enforcement investigators and commercial businesses do the same. It doesn't require breaking into anything; these agencies simply do what everybody else does: They're reading public forums. They're also doing something few others do: collecting and analyzing that data.

However, OSINT is far more than just search engines and social media. The topic is so vast that whole books are dedicated to explaining it, and numerous professionals (including my companies) consult on it. For this work, I cover just the basics:

The Intelligence Cycle

The process through which intelligence is obtained, produced, and shared employs six steps. The names and details vary from agency to agency; however, the process is largely the same.

1. Planning and Direction

One must first define the requirements and set the objectives for the process. Decision-makers identify what information is needed and prioritize those requirements based on strategic goals. Effective planning lays the foundation for the success of the intelligence cycle, ensuring that efforts remain focused and resources are allocated appropriately. Finally, the various collection assets and agencies are tasked with gathering the necessary information.

2. Collection

Gathering raw data and information from various sources now begins. The collected data may come from any of the tools noted above. The agencies' mandate includes collecting as much relevant information as possible to address the chosen intelligence requirements.

Documenting your processes goes hand-in-hand with collection. Keeping track of your strategies, sources, and findings aids in organization and refining your methods over time. Security and privacy must also be considered, especially when handling sensitive information. Using tools like VPNs and secured browsers and maintaining a cautious digital presence should be standard practices.

3. Processing

The raw data must now be converted into usable formats. This can include decryption, translation, data reduction, and data storage. The raw data is often voluminous and must be sorted and organized for usefulness. Irrelevant or redundant data is also filtered out at this stage. Processing ensures that the data is clean, structured, and prepared for analysis. Without it, making sense of the enormous amounts of information would be all-but-impossible.

4. Analysis

The core of the intelligence cycle answers questions among them:

- What does this data mean?
- How is it useful?
- What patterns, relationships, and trends does it show?
- Does this info confirm or undermine the accuracy of data gathered from other sources?

Analytical techniques and tools include general critical thinking skills combined with expertise in specific areas (economics, politics, sociology, technology, and others) to provide context and understanding. The analysis turns raw data into actionable intelligence by drawing conclusions and making predictions. These are then correlated into intelligence reports for decision-makers.

5. Dissemination

Finished intelligence products are distributed on a need-to-know basis. In the military, that's usually unit commanders and senior political policymakers. Security can be tight, meaning products might be passed around with the care and caution of Ebenezer Scrooge handing out gold coins. Dissemination can take various forms, such as written reports, briefings, or digital dashboards. It's essential that intelligence is presented clearly and concisely, emphasizing key findings and recommendations. Effective dissemination ensures that intelligence reaches the right people in a timely manner, enabling them to make informed, effective decisions.

6. Feedback

Finally, every operation must be evaluated for the efficiency of its collection and the quality of the resulting intelligence. Consumers of the intelligence provide feedback on the quality, relevance, and timeliness of the intelligence reports. This feedback is crucial for continuous improvement; it helps refine future intelligence requirements, adjust collection strategies, and enhance analytical methods. It ensures that the intelligence cycle remains dynamic and responsive to the evolving needs of decision-makers.

Real Life Tools

In corporations, non-governmental organizations (NGOs), and among private citizens, some appropriate OSINT-gathering tools (as of 2024) include:

- *Google Dorks*: For advanced Google searches to find hidden data. Utilize advanced search techniques to uncover information not easily accessible through standard search queries.

- *Maltego*: For mapping and visualizing relationships between entities. Create graphs showing relationships between people, companies, domains, and other entities. It's especially useful for detailed person or company investigations.
- *Recon-ng*: A full-featured web reconnaissance framework. Automate the process of gathering information from various sources and compiling it into a centralized database for analysis.
- *Shodan*: For finding information on internet-connected devices. Identify connected devices, such as servers and IoT devices, which might reveal vulnerabilities or detailed configuration information.
- *SpiderFoot*: Automated OSINT tool for threat intelligence. It also automates the process of gathering information from various sources and compiling it into a centralized database for analysis.
- *TOR*: a browser used to access the deep web.
- Even social media platforms—*LinkedIn*, *Facebook*, *X* (formerly Twitter), and others—can provide valuable personal and professional info.

Based on the analysis, one can then create strategies, goals, and action plans to mitigate risks or capitalize on opportunities.

Scenario 3: A Background Check

Perform a background check on a person being considered for a senior role in the mergers and acquisitions (M&A) division.

1. **Define Objectives**: Verify the individual's background, financial stability, and professional reputation.
2. **Gather Data**: *Maltego* maps the individual's connections to other entities and individuals. *LinkedIn* and other social media provide information on employment history, endorsements, and social activities, as well as connected members who could have posted pictures or other things with the person of interest. *Google Dorks* searches for specific terms related to the individual's name and potential red flags (e.g., lawsuits, financial troubles). *SpiderFoot* automates the collection of

detailed information from various sources (credit agencies, etc.). The *TOR* browser checks sources in the dark net.

3. **Analyze Data**: Cross-verify information, ensuring consistency across different data sources. Identify red flags, including any mentions of legal issues, financial problems, or negative professional feedback.
4. **Act on Intelligence**: Risk Assessment evaluates the potential risks associated with proceeding with the M&A.
5. **Decision-makers**: Decide whether to continue with, negotiate further terms with, or halt the M&A process based on the findings.

Scenario 4: A Supply Issue

A specific alloy is scarce on the global market but urgently needed.

1. **Define Objectives**: Identify potential suppliers or sources of the rare alloy urgently needed.
2. **Gather Data**: *Maltego* identifies companies and their connections to suppliers of the alloy. *Shodan* locates industrial facilities and companies dealing with that alloy, while *Google Dorks* finds less-publicized sources and suppliers. *Recon-ng* gathers detailed information on potential suppliers while TOR checks the dark net. *Hootsuite* and other social media outlets are examined for chatter about the alloy.
3. **Analyze Data**: The supplier evaluation team verifies the legitimacy and reliability of potential suppliers. The market trends team analyses developments and availability of the alloy in the global market.
4. **Act on Intelligence**: The supply department contacts potential suppliers to identify those willing to deal and negotiates terms to ensure the supply while establishing relationships with diverse sources and multiple suppliers to mitigate future risks.

Situational Awareness

Maintaining situational awareness can be a significant challenge in today's fast-paced and technologically driven world. Many people are so engrossed in their smartphones and digital lives that they often fail to recognize the physical realities around them. This lack of awareness can lead to disastrous consequences, especially during unexpected crises.

Importance

Situational awareness is the ability to perceive and understand the environment around you, comprehend the significance of what you observe, and predict how it might affect you. It's crucial to identify potential threats and crises before they escalate. Without situational awareness, individuals are like zombies, oblivious to the dangers they face, similar to those who, while engrossed in their smartphones, walk into walls, fall into rivers, or get hit by cars.

Missing the Mark

When people lack situational awareness, they miss crucial signs indicating an impending crisis. This unawareness can stem from a range of factors, all of which can hinder an individual's ability to recognize and respond to potential threats.

One common issue is distraction by technology. Many individuals focus so intently on their devices that they fail to notice changes in their environment. This distraction can cause them to miss visual and auditory cues that signal danger. Whether it's pedestrians walking into traffic while texting or someone not noticing a fire alarm because they're wearing headphones, technology can create significant blind spots.

Routine blindness can also lead to a lack of awareness. People become so accustomed to their daily routines that they overlook anomalies. This complacency can prevent them from recognizing when something is amiss. For example, an employee might ignore unusual behavior in the workplace because they are too focused on their regular tasks, missing early signs of a security breach.

Ignoring gut feelings is also a critical issue. Intuition often alerts us to potential dangers before our conscious mind can process them. However, many people dismiss these gut feelings, resulting in missed opportunities to avoid a crisis. For instance, a traveler might feel uneasy about a particular route but ignore this instinct, only to encounter trouble down the road.

Lastly, overconfidence can be an awareness killer. Some individuals believe that crises only happen to others, leading to a dangerous sense of invulnerability. Overconfident people might ignore warning signs, thinking they are immune to unexpected problems. This mindset can prevent them from taking necessary precautions and leave them unprepared when a crisis does occur.

Improving situational awareness involves being mindful of these tendencies and actively working to counteract them. By staying present, observing the environment, and trusting their instincts, individuals can better recognize and respond to potential threats, enhancing their overall safety and preparedness.

Few people, especially the bad guys, will go out of their way to share information with you. You need to look for it. Be proactive, or you will become reactive, leading to your organization becoming inactive.

Enhancing Awareness

Mindfulness practices, such as meditation or deep breathing techniques, can significantly enhance your awareness. You can stay present and focused by taking a few moments during your daily commute to practice deep breathing and observing your surroundings. Notice the people, sounds, and movements around you, which helps you stay grounded and alert.

Developing the habit of regularly scanning your environment is another effective strategy. This means consciously observing your surroundings to identify potential threats or changes. For instance, when you enter a new place, such as a restaurant or a public event, take a moment to identify exits, note the layout, and observe the behavior of people around you. This habit ensures you are always aware of your environment and can quickly adapt to any situation.

Mental scenario planning is a valuable technique where you visualize potential crises and plan your responses. While at work, imagine a scenario where there is a sudden fire alarm. Plan how you would evacuate, identify the nearest exits, and think about how you would help others in such a situation. This mental rehearsal prepares you for real-life emergencies by familiarizing you with potential responses.

Leveraging technology wisely can also enhance situational awareness. Use apps and tools to stay informed without becoming overly dependent on them. For example, a weather app can keep you updated on severe weather conditions while ensuring you're not glued to your smartphone, missing what's happening around you. Technology should enhance your awareness, not replace it.

Practicing the OODA Loop (Observe, Orient, Decide, Act) is a decision-making process that enhances situational awareness. While driving, continuously observe traffic conditions, understand the behavior of other drivers, decide on safe maneuvers, and execute those maneuvers. This systematic approach ensures you remain vigilant and responsive to changes in your environment—more details on this in Chapter 4.

Developing active listening skills is crucial for picking up on important verbal and nonverbal cues from others. In a meeting, focus on what colleagues are saying and how they are saying it. Pay attention to their tone, body language, and any underlying messages. This attentiveness helps you understand the full context of the conversation and respond appropriately.

Regularly changing your routine can help you avoid complacency and enhance alertness. Take different routes to work or vary your exercise routines. This keeps you from falling into autopilot mode and enables you to stay alert to changes or unusual activities in your environment.

Participating in training programs and simulations that mimic real-life crises can improve your response capabilities. Joining a first aid or self-defense class provides practical skills. It enhances your ability to remain aware and responsive in emergencies. This training prepares you for a variety of situations and builds your confidence in handling them.

Building observation skills through exercises like memory games or detailed noting of surroundings can sharpen your attention to detail. During a walk in the park, remember specific details like the number of benches, types of trees, or clothing of passersby. This practice improves your ability to notice and remember key details in your environment.

Finally, fostering collaborative awareness by working with others to share information can significantly improve situational awareness. In a workplace, create a culture where team members regularly share observations about safety, potential hazards, or unusual activities. This collaborative approach ensures that everyone stays informed and alert, enhancing the overall safety and responsiveness of the group.

By implementing these strategies, you can significantly enhance your situational awareness. This helps recognize potential crises and prepares you to respond effectively, ensuring your safety and well-being in various environments.

Situational awareness is crucial in preventing crises and ensuring safety. Here are some real-world examples where better awareness could have made a significant difference:

Historic Examples

Note: The following examples reflect actual events. The names of the corporations, individuals, and products have been altered and simplified to maintain client privacy.

Scenario 5: Tech Innovate's Success

Tech Innovate was preparing to launch a groundbreaking new application designed to revolutionize project management. The launch announcement was scheduled during a major industry conference, promising significant media coverage and customer engagement. Two weeks before the launch, the project manager, Susan, began to notice subtle signs of potential issues. Despite the development team's assurance that everything was on track, Susan observed that some team members appeared unusually stressed and overheard discussions about unanticipated technical challenges. She organized a series of informal meetings and one-on-one discussions with team members to gather more detailed insights. She also reviewed the project's timeline, checking for discrepancies between reported progress and actual milestones.

Susan discovered that a critical component of the application was not integrating as seamlessly as expected with existing systems. The lead developer admitted (privately) that the team had underestimated the complexity of this integration. She escalated the issue and called for "air support" immediately, convening a crisis management meeting with the development team and senior leadership. They immediately allocated additional resources and brought in an external specialist to address the integration issue.

Susan's situational awareness was nothing more than paying attention to what was happening around her. Specifically:

1. Susan gathered intelligence. People handle stress differently; to know that her team was stressed, she had to know her team. That allowed her to see that they were not at their best.
2. She admitted there was a problem. She saw the signs and assumed the worst, then talked to her people, as a group and one-on-one, to confirm her suspicions.
3. She communicated transparently with stakeholders, the team, and management. She explained the situation and the steps being taken to resolve it.
4. They developed a course of action. In this case, the team needed more people and some outside advice to get them back on track.
5. She adjusted the plan. In this case, the calendar was the defining factor; they needed to launch on a specific date. Less time, they decided, required more people to get the job done.

Susan's situational awareness and proactive management allowed Tech Innovate to address the technical challenges before the launch. The application launched successfully, receiving positive feedback and achieving high customer satisfaction. This reinforced the company's reputation for reliability and quality. Had Susan not been paying attention, the outcome could have been dire.

Scenario 6: Retail Haven's Failure

Retail Haven, a popular retail chain, enjoyed a period of rapid expansion. With a strong customer base and increasing profits, the company decided to open ten new locations within six months. Amidst the expansion frenzy, Emma, a mid-level manager, noticed several key performance indicators (KPIs) began to show troubling trends. Customer satisfaction scores were dipping, and employee turnover rates were rising. She shared her concerns with corporate headquarters, who remained focused on growth, viewing Emma's observations as temporary setbacks.

Within a year, Retail Haven began facing significant backlash. Customer complaints on social media grew more numerous, leading to widespread negative publicity. Employee dissatisfaction resulted in high turnover, creating staffing issues. The ten new locations struggled to attract and retain customers, and sales company-wide began to decline. Eventually, Retail Haven was forced to close several stores, and the company's reputation suffered a severe blow.

Corporate's neglect of situational awareness allowed minor issues to escalate into major crises, jeopardizing the company's long-term success. Specifically:

1. Corporate ignoring early warnings. Emma had intelligence that should've raised concerns, but headquarters continued emphasizing the importance of meeting expansion targets and refused to address issues in existing locations.
2. Lack of proactivity. Headquarters didn't investigate the root causes of declining customer satisfaction and increasing employee turnover. They failed to allocate resources for training or improving working conditions. They assumed these issues would resolve themselves.
3. Failure to adapt. A rigid adherence to a plan meant no adjustments were allowed to address new challenges—a significant disconnect developed between the executive suite's perception and reality.

Retail Haven is not alone; history is rich with examples. In the 1990s and early 2000s, everybody (myself included) had a Nokia cellphone. Their market share was huge. Then, along came the iPhone, and Nokia collapsed. (Some insiders later claimed that upper-echelon management rejected many potential innovations, instead relying on past successes.) The "Nokia Effect" has come to describe a company's quick downfall. The mobile phone industry was changing rapidly in the 1990s and 2000s, and I'm fairly convinced that corporate's lack of situational awareness left them flying blind. By 2014, Nokia's global brand value had fallen almost to the bottom of the Top 100.

Scenario 7: AutoTech's Success

AutoTech, a renowned car manufacturer, was preparing to launch a new electric vehicle (EV) model that promised to set new standards in their industry. The success of this launch depended heavily on a steady supply of high-quality batteries from their primary supplier, PowerCellz. Three months before the launch, James, AutoTech's supply chain manager, noticed minor delays in deliveries from PowerCellz. Although the delays were within acceptable limits, James investigated further. He met with key managers at PowerCellz to discuss the delays and understand the underlying issues. He also reviewed recent market trends and news related to battery production and raw material availability.

PowerCellz was experiencing a temporary shortage of critical raw materials due to geopolitical tensions in their supplier's country. The length and scope of delays caused by this shortage were unknown and could potentially cause significant delays if the issues were not resolved.

Since PowerCellz's supply of that raw material was outside their control, James and his team worked with PowerCellz to identify alternative material sources and streamline logistics to mitigate the impact of the shortage. Since PowerCellz was outside his control, James also diversified AutoTech's supplier base, engaging a secondary battery supplier as a contingency.

James then communicated the situation and his strategies to AutoTech's senior management, ensuring everyone was aligned. Their production schedule required slight adjustments to accommodate the new supply chain dynamics. Still, those changes did not compromise the launch timeline.

James' proactivity killed a crisis while it was still a barely noticeable problem. Specifically:

1. James gathered intelligence. Seeing a situation that wasn't, strictly speaking, a problem, James did research that demonstrated a potentially severe problem existed.
2. He admitted that a crisis was coming. He discussed the issues with PowerCellz, who may have been denying the reality of the situation.
3. He developed, with other stakeholders, a course of action. He assisted his supplier in dealing with their supplier while

making other arrangements in case his supplier's efforts failed to resolve the situation.

4. He communicated and adjusted. He took his concerns to the source and informed his superiors of his proposed solution. They were then able to adjust their schedule to meet the new situation.

Thanks to James' situational awareness and effective management, AutoTech successfully navigated the potential supply chain disruption. The new EV model launched on time, receiving praise for its innovation and reliability. AutoTech's ability to foresee and address supply chain risks reinforced its reputation as a resilient and forward-thinking manufacturer.

Scenario 8: Metro Motors' Failure

Metro Motors, a major car manufacturer, was on the verge of launching a new luxury sedan model. The success of this model hinged on the timely and quality delivery of an advanced infotainment system from an outside supplier, TekConnekt.

Six weeks before the scheduled launch, Sarah, Metro Motors' supply chain coordinator, began receiving reports on quality issues and delays with the infotainment systems from the assembly line. The initial feedback indicated minor malfunctions, but Sarah's attempts to escalate these concerns to senior management were largely ignored.

The Metro Motors' executive suite prioritized the launch timeline over a "supposed" quality issue. Sarah's observations and recommendations for a thorough inspection were dismissed as an overreaction. No additional quality checks or audits were authorized, and no potential backup suppliers were contacted. TekConnekt wasn't even informed of their infotainment center's problems.

As the launch date approached, the extent of the quality issues with the infotainment systems became evident. Several vehicles had to be recalled due to system failures, leading to a significant delay in the launch.

Had Sarah's warnings been heeded, Metro Motors wouldn't have lost sales and reputation. Specifically:

1. Sarah provided an early warning of a potentially severe problem, but the executive suite ignored her.
2. Metro Motors refused to enact proactive measures. No tests were made on incoming parts. They refused to interact with TekConnekt to correct the problem in TekConnekt's factory.
3. The company failed to adapt, relying solely on TekConnekt instead of pursuing alternatives. The company fixed its launch date, refusing to allocate resources for troubleshooting or contingency planning.

Communications broke down among departments, escalating the issue and leaving the quality concerns unaddressed. Missing the launch date generated significant negative media backlash, damaging Metro Motors' reputation. The results were lost customer confidence, a sharp decline in sales, and a stock price drop.

Review

None of these situations were unusual in any way. A company should expect a glitch or two in innovative technology. "Growing pains" are common as companies expand. Supply chain issues happen—more often when multiple supplier-customer relationships exist or raw materials cross international boundaries. Complex mechanisms with numerous sub-assemblies often don't integrate perfectly until installed, evaluated for compatibility, and attuned.

As I noted earlier, what we see is often what we want to see, not what we should be seeing. Proper intelligence gathering gives decision-makers the data they need to project outcomes and consequences. Knowing the consequences allows them to choose among the alternatives and create the best-case scenario. Sometimes, it allows them to head off a crisis before anyone outside the executive suite knows it's on the horizon.

Situational awareness begins with knowing that potential threats exist. It moves through proactively looking for those threats and preparing to meet them. It ends with successfully preserving value. We shall deal with all three aspects in the coming pages.

Special Case: Cybersecurity

The biggest threat to any average business today is that we put everything we can into cyberspace, the net, or the cloud. Online and remote work has saved so much time, effort, and labor that their use may very well increase. Vigilance, therefore, must also increase. The attacks vary and include uploading malware to your system to damage it or erase data; denial-of-service attacks flooding your servers with so many false orders that your system becomes clogged; phishing and spoofing to indirectly obtain information; hacking into your system to directly steal data; ransomware that shuts down your system unless you pay up; to name a few.

For every attack type, we have defensive software available. Your best defense, however, is employees who see problems early and avoid accidentally helping the bad players. Cybersecurity should be part of your ongoing training program.

Making The Admission

Once you've admitted the crisis to yourself and begun to fight it, others may need to know the situation.

To Those with Need-to-Know

In the QCo example, the business lost its largest customer. Few businesses are large enough or so well known that the person on the street cares for or pays attention to. That said, assume that a part of the public does care about you and will find out about your situation quickly. You must prepare to meet their questions and concerns with good answers and a plan of action.

So, who needs to know? (And we are defining "need" as narrowly as possible in the initial stages of the situation.) Certainly, the list includes the owners of a small private company or the executive team in a larger business—whoever will have the final say in managing the crisis. The managers of the specific department or project will (or should) have the best intelligence on the situation. You may also include your quality control staff, accountants and lawyers, engineers, or anyone else who can provide real intelligence as to the problem, the consequences, the remedies, and other mitigation factors.

Whoever you need to call, call them quickly and carefully get to work.

To Stakeholders

Continuing our AA component example from another perspective: When that customer called to say, "Your parts are substandard, I'm not going to buy from you anymore," every stakeholder in the business—all those who deal directly with QCo—could be hurt by this situation, and some of them could be able to help QCo out of it.

Any stakeholders not directly involved in this supplier-user relationship—those who don't buy the AA—may hear about this situation through the grapevine or some other source. Even though other QCo customers aren't directly involved, this is intelligence. As stakeholders, what happens to QCo affects them. In most situations, they can't fix QCo's problem, but they can (and might) walk away from it by severing their ties with QCo. (If their intelligence gathering determines that QCo won't survive this crisis, they'd be fools not to act in their best interest.)

These other customers may call to ask some tough questions so they can determine if QCo is still a supplier they want to do business with. QCo must admit that a crisis exists and explain, in part, at least, what they're doing to solve the crisis. Their goal will be to convince each customer to stay with them. QCo will, of course, downplay the magnitude of the issue. They'll give assurances that their other products are of quality and that QCo isn't going under despite the loss of a major client.

Regardless of the outcome of this intelligence gathering, those other customers may still err on the side of caution and drop QCo as their supplier. They may not feel they can take chances. Equally possible, QCo might be a long-term partner reliably providing good products. If that customer decides the problem is short-term, they may decide they need to support QCo (which is a stakeholder in their company) and help them through this crisis.

To the Public

We discuss private affairs in public only when unavoidable.

In America, laws on public disclosure by publicly traded companies (those that issue stock) are very clear. Violations are prosecuted vigorously, as they may constitute fraud.

As noted above, failure to publicly disclose facts surrounding risks to public safety is treated very seriously, both in criminal and civil law.

Only the people at the center of a crisis or potential crisis can properly decide to share with the public, when to share, and how much to share.

Knowing and Facing the Situation

A corporate crisis is a time of intense difficulty characterized by tremendous uncertainty. Human responses within companies in crisis are complex and varied, influenced by personality, experience, culture, and one's role in the organization. The survival instinct can manifest rationally or irrationally, impacting decisions and resolution efforts.

In my experience, once the group had accepted that a crisis is in progress, individuals typically go through several psychological stages in response to crises. As noted earlier, the initial shock can lead to denial. Eventually, though, nobody can avoid the fact that a crisis exists.

Strong emotional responses typically follow—generally a bad state of mind for decision-making. As the crisis progresses, many move toward adaptation—management and employees begin working to cope. Eventually, people realize that significant post-traumatic growth is possible. Once that sinks in, the organization can become energized to solve problems, with the company emerging stronger with greater resilience against future crises.

In any context (corporate or personal), behavior during crises significantly impacts outcomes. Groups can provide needed mutual support. They can also be susceptible to collective panic, rash decision-making, or groupthink. I've found that culture plays a leading role in shaping group dynamics. Effective crisis management supports constructive group dynamics, mitigates counterproductive behaviors, and accounts for the unique aspects of each organization's culture and structure.

Examples

Some time ago, my team was engaged to manage a supplier of electrical components that entered insolvency proceedings after more than 12 months of struggle. Seeing the handwriting on the wall, many employees left to seek work elsewhere. The majority remained working and hopeful, only to be shocked by the court's announcement of the insolvency procedure.

There was significant resentment toward management and owners, and employees feared losing their jobs. Despite the uncertain future, the employees persevered and performed their usual duties. After more than ten months of searching, we secured a financially robust multinational investor. This period of adversity forged strong bonds among the staff, leading to significant innovations that secured orders for years ahead. Those who endured the ordeal were substantially rewarded for their faith and resilience.

Another recent project involved managing a car accessory manufacturer in crisis. The company's owners embezzled corporate funds and fled the country, leaving the business in dire straits. Leaderless, the employees faced an uncertain future until we intervened in conjunction with a car manufacturer and the local court. We were able to continue production with funds from their principal client while we sought an investor.

The crisis also unmasked two middle managers exploiting the situation for personal gain by spreading misinformation and fueling division. By exposing and dismissing these jackals, we restored group unity and eventually secured a successful investor takeover.

These events underscore the critical role of leadership in managing group dynamics and ensuring organizational resilience amidst crises.

Building Resilience

Cultivating a Crisis-Ready Culture

A crisis-ready culture enables businesses not only to survive but also thrive in the face of unexpected challenges. The global challenges are severe, and there is no doubt that there is potential for surprises and crises on both macro and micro levels.

Being the CEO of a company that provides crisis management services to the automotive space, here are the strategies I recommend all companies keep in mind to cultivate a culture that is prepared for and can effectively respond to crises.

Crisis-Ready Organizations

A crisis-ready culture is characterized by its adaptability, proactive mindset, and forceful communication channels. Organizations with such a culture are better equipped to oversee disruptions, maintain operations, and recover quickly from setbacks. In my experience, companies with a crisis-ready culture can see increased employee morale, faster recovery times, and sustained business operations even in the most challenging circumstances. Some of the elements that are essential to building this type of culture include:

1. Leadership Commitment

Leadership plays a pivotal role in establishing a crisis-ready culture. Leaders must model resilience and a proactive approach to crisis management. This involves demonstrating calmness under pressure, making informed decisions quickly, and communicating transparently with all stakeholders.

I believe leaders such as Mary Barra, CEO of General Motors, and Satya Nadella, CEO of Microsoft, have successfully guided their organizations through crises by embodying these qualities. As I see it, their commitment to resilience has set a tone that permeates their companies.

In my experience as a crisis manager in the field, I have seen managers that lacked those attributes. Recently, a CEO of a company in turmoil mentioned in a meeting with his team that he wishes "to get knocked out and wake up when the crisis is over." This was the moment he lost his leadership team. The company did not survive.

2. Employee Engagement and Empowerment

Involving employees at all levels in crisis preparedness is crucial. Empower employees to take initiative during a crisis. This can significantly enhance an organization's response capabilities. To do so, provide regular training and opportunities for continuous learning and ensure your employees are equipped with any necessary skills and knowledge. I've found that encouraging a sense of ownership and accountability also fosters a more engaged and proactive workforce.

3. Communication and Transparency

Effective communication is the backbone of crisis management. Establishing clear and open communication channels ensures information flows seamlessly throughout the organization.

Transparency is equally important; keeping employees and stakeholders informed with regular updates builds trust and fosters a collaborative environment.

However, it is always important for leaders to ensure they don't give up tactical advantage by communicating too openly. It is a delicate line, and if in doubt, and depending on the vastness of the crisis, get professionals and lawyers on the crisis management team to avoid fatal—and expensive—mistakes.

4. Continuous Improvement and Learning

A crisis-ready culture thrives on continuous improvement and learning. Organizations should regularly review and learn from past crises and near-misses to enhance their preparedness. Implementing feedback loops and encouraging a culture of continuous improvement can help organizations stay ahead of potential threats. For example, I believe Toyota's commitment to continuous improvement can allow the company to refine its crisis management strategies and ensure better preparedness for future challenges.

5. Building Strong Relationships and Networks

Strong relationships and networks are vital for effective crisis management. Internal collaboration and external partnerships can provide additional resources and support during crises. Building robust relationships with suppliers, customers, regulatory bodies, and other stakeholders ensure a more coordinated and effective response. For example, Google leverages an extensive network to provide essential information during crises, according to the company's Crisis Response page. This demonstrates the power of strong relationships.

6. Scenario Planning and Simulations

Conduct regular scenario planning sessions to anticipate potential crises and develop appropriate response strategies. Simulations help evaluate these strategies in a controlled environment so organizations can identify gaps and areas for improvement. Common crisis scenarios, such as natural disasters, cyberattacks, and supply chain disruptions, can be prepared for through diligent scenario planning.

7. Integrating Crisis Management into Daily Operations

To ensure readiness becomes a part of the organizational fabric, I recommend integrating crisis management practices into daily operations. Aligning crisis management with overall business goals and objectives reinforces its importance and encourages a culture of readiness. This involves incorporating risk assessments, emergency response plans, and business continuity strategies into everyday activities.

For example, regarding risk assessments, companies can hold daily safety meetings and conduct monthly risk audits. Once an emergency response plan has been established, businesses should provide employee training, establish emergency kits and stations, and develop communication protocols. Finally, companies can prioritize data backups and IT resilience to support business continuity, diversify their suppliers, and plan for different scenarios. Because our core business is risk mitigation and crisis management, we use these types of tools daily. Efforts like these help ensure crisis management is not an afterthought but a fundamental aspect of operations.

8. Measuring and Monitoring Resilience

Measuring and monitoring organizational resilience is crucial for continuous improvement. Track key performance indicators and metrics, such as response times, recovery rates, and employee readiness, help assess progress, and identify areas for enhancement. Furthermore, regularly review and update crisis management plans and procedures to ensure they remain relevant and effective in today's ever-changing landscape.

A Call to Action

Business leaders should take proactive steps to assess their organization's current crisis readiness. Using available resources and tools, they can begin the journey toward building and maintaining a crisis-ready culture that ensures resilience and adaptability in the face of any challenge.

Incorporating these strategies can not only prepare businesses for crises but also create a more dynamic, agile, and forward-thinking organization that's ready to seize opportunities and overcome obstacles.

Chapter 3

Analyze the Threat

Threat Analysis—Is It a Crisis?

After gathering intelligence, the data must be properly analyzed. Only then can you know if it is actionable information or distractive data—not pertinent to the current situation. At this stage, analysis passes beyond inspection of the data. It includes assessing potential risks and opportunities that might follow using the data and considering alternative scenarios to make informed decisions.

Scenario 9: Shock and Awe—The Life-or-Death Situation

Some years ago, in the United States, a maniac took several guns to a shopping mall and, after spending an hour in a restroom, exited into the food court, opening fire on innocent shoppers. (Ultimately, he fired 24 shots, killing three shoppers and wounding two more.) As the first shots were fired, another shopper, armed with a legally owned and carried pistol, returned fire while shouting for others to get behind him. Though neither a military service member nor a law enforcement officer, the 22-year-old put eight of his ten rounds into the maniac from 40 yards away, killing him. According to surveillance video later viewed by millions, from the moment the shooter opened the restroom door until he was dead was exactly 15 seconds.

As you'd expect, the young man was interviewed by many media outlets over the following weeks. Asked where he got his firearms training, the young man credited his grandfather as his instructor.

In this case, the analysis was as simple as could be—this was a clear and present danger, and deadly force was employed. Military personnel, law enforcement officers, public safety personnel, and medical practitioners face these crises daily. They must make almost instant decisions based on whatever intelligence their senses can gather in about the time it takes to turn your head 180 degrees. These professionals don't need tools but muscle memory and trained instincts.

For this reason, a significant part of their training is spent in simulations. Agencies recreate, as closely as possible, major threat scenarios—gunmen, fires, earthquakes, infectious diseases, bombings, and more—so their people don't have to think about what they need to do. Instinct and muscle memory take over, and they can proactively deal with situations instead of reacting to them.

In a business or family, that level of threat is rare. Many of us will never see such a situation except on the evening news. However, business offices, factories, stores, and homes catch fire. Computers get hacked. Cancers strike. Businesses have "reductions in force" or close outright. Cars crash into cars, streetlights, and other things. Even the seemingly perfect life can be thrown into chaos in the blink of an eye.

In these cases, your intelligence gathering and course of action planning must precede the crisis to be most effective. The tools are the same for a large or small business, a community, or an individual. The details differ, but the principles are universal. The key is time—how much do you have from the moment the crisis is identified until you need to act to resolve it?

Time is vital to deciding how to apply your tools to your circumstances. Until the crisis arises, you have time to prepare. Reading this book, checking relevant websites, and taking classes in firearms safety, first aid, earthquake or blizzard, or forest fire prep, depending on your locale, could mean the difference between getting through a disaster and losing everything you hold dear.

Scenario 10: The Clock is Ticking

In an other-than-life-and-death situation, you have time; use it!

Let's say that our friends at QCo solved their model AA problem, and things have gone back to normal for several months. Then, unexpectedly, they get a call from SpecFast, their supplier of specialty fasteners. They informed QCo that their business was closing down. "We're sorry, but we've been hit by a disaster. We are going out of business and can do nothing to stop it. We've shut down all operations, and we don't see any way we'll be able to restart."

Your one piece of good luck in this is that the threat analysis was complete before that phone call ended. QCo, you have a crisis on your hands. You need intelligence and a course of action. Intelligence, I remind you, is actionable information obtained by asking the right questions.

As QCo proceeds to deal with the SpecFast situation, it needs to remember the five foundational attitudes of successful crisis management:

1. Get a Grip, Keep a Grip.
2. Keep it Simple.
3. Act Decisively.
4. Be Unstoppable.
5. End the Threat.

Your most vital data will be your parts inventory. Had I been the QCo operations manager, my first question to SpecFast—during that initial phone call—would be, "How many of our fasteners do you have onsite right now? I'll buy them all unless they're committed to other customers." That's the instinct and muscle memory kicking in—you got it, I need it, hand it over, here's my check! (You'll let accounting figure out how to pay for it later.)

They have some and send them over. The inventory manager determines that QCo now has a 30-day supply of this fastener at a normal usage rate. (Remember that phrase, "normal rate of usage." That will figure into your course of action.) The ops manager (now bearing the added title "crisis manager") has the key to their whole **A.D.M.I.T.** development—the timeline is six business weeks. The manager now gathers those with need-to-know:

- The operations manager will form and chair the crisis management team.
- The supply manager will be watching the inventory.
- The engineering manager will be providing technical information for potential replacements.
- The accountant will be figuring out the costs of resolving the crisis.
- The owner (onsite or offsite) will be regularly updated to be ready to act when decisions are needed.
- And such others as have that need-to-know.

Next comes intelligence gathering. Complete information—as complete as you can gather in the time allotted—will give decision-makers the data they need to project outcomes and consequences.

Let's say that experience shows you only need one week from order to delivery by SpecFast. The team decides they must have a plan in place in four weeks to give the new supplier plenty of time to complete and deliver their first order. Calendars are marked, and research begins on the alternatives:

Alternative 1—Continuation

Is SpecFast really dead or just severely wounded? I mentioned earlier that every company that does business with you is your stakeholder. Sometimes, a stakeholder must walk away from your crisis to save their business, but occasionally, they can save yours instead.

QCo has been buying SpecFast fasteners for a while, and QCo likes their operation—they deliver on time without quality issues and charge a fair price. Can QCo absorb SpecFast? This is owner-to-owner territory. Mr. QCo will discuss with Mrs. SpecFast the possibility of a merger or, perhaps, purchasing their shop and equipment and hiring some of their workers or some other scenario. How much of SpecFast's business was QCo? What disaster is taking them down? What alternatives have they examined to save their business? What would it cost QCo? Should they be run as separate companies under one corporate ownership or integrated? How will other SpecFast customers react? Will they continue to buy?

These are just a few among a long list of questions. Getting all those answers, making decisions, and completing contracts in about a month would be a considerable challenge. But, in the end, does the potential profit outweigh the costs and risks?

Alternative 2—Ask for Help

"Don't reinvent the wheel" is among our most common axioms. Why do work that others have already done?

If SpecFast's fasteners weren't a custom item for QCo, they're selling it to other companies. Perhaps some of those others would want to take part in a joint venture to keep SpecFast afloat. If not, ask those companies if they have an alternative source or know of possible other sources with a good reputation.

Maybe other companies in the market aren't using a SpecFast fastener but are using something similar. They could be surveyed for potential new suppliers or a whole new fastener.

Alternative 3—Find Your Own Answers

While those discussions happen, engineering and supply are on the internet and the phones with other potential suppliers. Intelligence gathering will tell you if there's another company that manufactures the same part with the exact technical specifications. Can this new supplier deliver parts within the six-week window at a good price?

They're also searching the market for alternative parts that fit within the technical specifications QCo needs. These potential suppliers are then questioned about specifications, tolerances, costs, delivery schedules, and so on.

At the same time, the sales staff talks to the customers. QCo might start supplying them with a product that has changed in terms of material. Do they approve of this possible new alternative or will changes to QCo's product mean technical issues for them? They might need to validate that the potential new product meets their needs—that adds time to the entire process and could change the pricing structure.

Consequences

Had I been asked, I would've reminded QCo that the law of unintended consequences is still on the books—right next to Murphy's Law. This whole scenario started with an unforeseen phone call or email. There may be more surprises lurking around the next corner. Once again, that measured paranoia has saved many. In any crisis, you are vulnerable. On today's mostly civilized planet Earth, we should not forget that vultures still circle dying animals, waiting for their next feast.

I advise using a structured hierarchy to make decisions. Like the branches of a tree, each decision has others to follow. Police detectives investigating a crime begin by assuming everyone might be guilty. They then gather evidence, which moves some people off the suspect list and others up the list until just one remains. Remember:

> Exclude the impossible, and what is left, however improbable, must be the truth.
>
> —Sir Arthur Conan Doyle[8]

Remember that whichever of these (or other) alternatives QCo chooses will have positive and negative repercussions. Time must be used efficiently. We always choose the alternative that we feel will create the best-case scenario. Still, we always watch how events unfold and adjust as needed—more on this later.

Mapping the Crisis: Tools for Comprehensive Analysis

1. "Proximal" Cause versus "Ultimate" Cause

> It isn't that they can't see the solution. It is that they can't see the problem.
>
> —Gilbert Keith Chesterton[9]

In US law, the ***proximal cause*** of a situation is ***what happened***. For example, a young man and a young woman drive their cars into trees. Local laws require a blood test to determine sobriety, so the police or medical personnel administer the test. In both cases, the

[8] Sir Arthur Conan Doyle, "The Fate of the Evangeline," *The Boy's Own Paper*. London: The Religious Tract Society, Christmas Issue, 1885. (Contrary to popular myth, it wasn't first spoken by Sherlock Holmes, it first appeared in a Holmes story five years later.)

[9] Gilbert Keith "G. K." Chesterton, *The Scandal of Father Brown*, London: Cassell and Company, 1935.

tests are positive. The drivers are arrested and charged with driving under the influence.

The ***ultimate cause*** of a situation is ***why it happened***. In the case of the young man, he was out with his fraternity brothers, and they got into a drinking contest. Being young and foolish, he decided he wasn't too drunk to drive home. He was wrong and will face stiff penalties. In the case of the young woman, her drink was tampered with—"roofied." Before the drug could take full effect, before she was even aware of the tampering, she realized her date was not her type and headed for home. Unfortunately, the drug took effect before she was safely in her apartment, and she lost consciousness. She will face no penalty, as the accident was due to circumstances beyond her control, but the guy who roofied her drink (if it can be proven he did) may be held civilly liable for all damage her accident caused and criminally liable for his assault on her.

Outside legal circles, the ultimate cause is often called the root cause. Root cause analyses (RCAs) are designed to identify the ultimate sources of the problem. Without getting to those roots, the correct solutions cannot be identified. RCA can progress more quickly and effectively by pairing an Ishikawa diagram with other tools to empirically investigate the failure. Often, failure investigations begin with brainstorming possible causes and listing them in an Ishikawa diagram. This focuses the crisis team on potential root causes and eliminates possibilities that couldn't have caused the problem and, therefore, would be distractions.

2. The "5 Why" Method

Scenario 11: Pizza

Getting to the heart of a crisis means asking questions. In many cases, one question, "Why?" must be asked five times before you get to the real problem. (Statistics show that investigations often don't reach the right answer until after the fifth "why.")

Let's take the example of a pizzeria owner. I drop in one evening and order a pizza, which comes to me burnt and inedible. I ask "Why?" five times:

1. "Why is the pizza burnt?" It was too long in the oven.

2. "Why was it too long in the oven?" Because the cook didn't take it out on time.
3. "Why didn't the cook take it out on time?" Because the timer stopped working.
4. "Why did the timer stop working?" Because the battery died.
5. "Why did the battery die?" Because the lunch shift manager failed to replace the battery or report to the dinner shift manager that the battery was low.

This is a simplistic scenario, but the point is there. You must keep asking probing questions to get to the root or underlying problem. Only when you reach the root is the crisis defined and assessed.

Scenario 12: Car Seats

Instead of pizza, let's assume I supply car seats to a major auto manufacturer. They called to inform me that we may have a serious crisis brewing. Two people were killed in an accident because the brackets holding the car seats to the frame broke, and the passengers were smashed into the steering wheel and dashboard. The automaker thinks that my company caused the problem.

I ask "Why?" five times:

1. "Why did the seat not hold?" The seat didn't hold because the brackets broke.
2. "Why did the brackets break?" My engineers examined the brackets and compared them to the design specifications. All seats are being built correctly, and the design has passed all tests for front-end crashes. So, we don't know.
3. "Why could they fail if they were designed and built correctly?" My engineers assumed the worst—because these specific seats were not built correctly.
4. "Why were these specific seats not built correctly?" The engineers got hold of a couple of cars with seats of the same lot as those that failed. Upon closer examination, the steel in the seat brackets was the wrong alloy.
5. "Why did our bracket supplier use the wrong alloy?' Because they were trying to save money.

This sort of tragedy happens too often; it's called "cutting corners." Everybody assumes they won't get caught. They're usually wrong, but not always, so people keep doing it. Now that we have the root problem, we can solve it and the crisis.

Human or Technical Error?

In both of these examples, you'll notice that the ultimate cause of the crisis was human error. Is the answer to the fifth "Why?" always a human error? Not necessarily, but it often is. Computer-controlled machines are increasing in terms of their abilities and popularity. Computers have a major positive—they do exactly what we tell them to do. Computers also have a major negative—they do exactly what we ask. Always remember that technical errors might be human errors in disguise.

Sometimes, you need just four; sometimes, you go to six, but on average, five of the right questions get to the root of the problem.

Risk Assessment—Key Components

Risk assessment stands as a cornerstone of strategic business decision-making. It, therefore, demands a structured and meticulous approach to ensure effectiveness.

1. Identify

At the heart of this process is the task of identifying risks. Once again, part of that identification is differentiating between symptoms of problems and the root cause of problems. This involves recognizing reality and clearly describing potential outcomes with the positives and negatives a business might face. The earlier a business recognizes these risks, the more power this determination bestows on the business.

2. Quantify

Once identified, businesses need to quantify the risks, gauging both their potential impact and likelihood.

Employing tools such as statistical modeling, analyses of historical data, and simulated scenarios provide valuable insights. Through this quantification, businesses can discern which threats merit immediate attention and which ones can be set aside for later.

3. Prioritize

Once quantified, businesses must deal with the risks carrying the greatest or the most immediate threat. Intelligence gathering provides businesses with data that allows them to rank the identified risks and determine which should be addressed first based on their significance.

Risk matrices compare the likelihood of a specific risk against its potential impact. They can play a crucial role in this assessment. For example, some risks (a cash-flow slowdown) take time to develop into a crisis. Other risks (such as an employee walkout) pose an immediate threat. It's essential to ensure the most significant risks are addressed immediately, focusing resources for maximum efficacy.

4. Evaluate

Once risk priorities are set, each risk must be comprehensively evaluated. Compare industry benchmarks, past experiences, or predetermined thresholds to decide the most appropriate way to address each threat. Assessment is pivotal in ensuring that risk management efforts remain in harmony with the company's long-term objectives and risk tolerance levels.

5. Mitigate and Manage

Tactical or short-term decisions begin immediately to repair damage or replace resources, while strategic or long-term decisions come into play to prevent future recurrences. Businesses can sometimes transfer risk through insurance, change their business processes, and/or put safeguards in place to diminish the risk's effect.

Effective risk management, in this regard, becomes a dual-edged sword; while it safeguards against potential adversities, it can also pave the way for opportunities, enabling growth and improvement.

Scenario 13: The Spy Among Us Is Us

A friend attends a security seminar on industrial espionage. Examples of successful infiltrations of companies in my industry are presented. That friend then sent me information on this threat. I decided to test my internal security by hiring an outside firm to get into my office and plant a listening device.

Plan A: One day, this person arrives at my office posing as a delivery driver and tells my gatekeeper at the front desk, "Oh, I have to hand it off personally." The front desk person says, "The CEO is not here, and I'm authorized to sign for all packages." FAIL!

My internal security protocols worked.

Plan B: The outside firm's operative plays an electrician and tells the front desk, "I need to go to this office to check the sockets." The front desk hasn't heard any complaints, but viewing this as a routine maintenance issue, the front desk gives this supposed craftsman access, and the device is planted. SUCCESS!

My internal protocols did not consider the ruse of a routine maintenance issue by the building's owner.

Review: I was informed of a possible threat—industrial espionage. The information included sufficient evidence to conclude that it was a credible, immediate threat with potentially severe consequences. Needing to act quickly, I set up a security test. A failure was followed by a success, so I rewrote the office SOPs to include a phone call to the building manager or requiring a written work order before any trade is allowed into my workspace.

Who is Affected and How?

When a crisis arises, everybody falls into one of two categories: Someone who could help or someone who could hurt our recovery. Who is which?

Scenario 14: The Farmers' Market

Identifying Key Stakeholders

Let's say I own a small farmer's market with a cash flow or liquidity problem. Who are my stakeholders?

- The other owners, if any.
- The employees.
- The customers.
- The suppliers whose products fill my shelves—wholesalers, farmers, and ranchers.

- The vendors with products and services I need to operate my business—my accountant, lawyer, paper bag maker, utility companies, landlord (if I lease my building), and bank (if I have a mortgage).
- And so on.

Assessing the Impact on Each Stakeholder Group

Let's look at the bank specifically: If I have a cash flow problem, the bank could be a major help or hindrance to my success in coming through this crisis. I have a $500,000 mortgage with them, which I've paid down steadily, with no problems, to $400,000.

The crisis team comprises the partners who own the business, plus their accountants, bankers, and lawyers. They look at all the data they have.

The banker considers: If the bank loans the market an additional $50,000, the bank may save the market in the short term, but can that business add this much to its debt load and continue to service that debt in the long term? If the market goes out of business, the bank may get a building it can sell to recover the money. Then again, it might not sell, and there may be no buyer. Can the bank afford to deal with a loss of $450,000? Would that cause a crisis for the bank? Would losing this local merchant cause undue strain on the customers or the town's general economy?

The accountant analyzes the books, which show a strong cash flow. Why is this problem arising now? The accountant reports that the market supplies several local restaurants, and they have been slow to pay their bills recently. The market now faces insufficient cash for payroll and utilities this month. That $50,000 would cover both months, giving the market time to collect past-due bills. Is that enough? What happens if the market sues the restaurants over past due amounts? The lawyer examines that scenario and reports it would take too much time, with considerable risk that the market doesn't win the suit or legal fees would drive the restaurants into bankruptcy or something. This is not an option with a high probability of success.

Acting on the Intelligence

The bank and market talk to the restaurant owners and discuss their situations. All, except one, give the team reason to believe their cash flow problems will be solved within two months and their accounts with the market will be up to date. Assuming that one remains far in arrears, can the market meet its obligations? It will be tight, the accountant says, but yes. The lawyer drafts agreements with each restaurant, lays out a payment schedule, and the restaurants sign.

With these assurances and documents in place, the bank loans the stop-gap funds. The market goes on with business as usual, and the other stakeholders—customers, suppliers, vendors, and so on—never even knew what happened. This success story had a flow:

- Intelligence was gathered, and a crisis management team came together.
- The situation was clearly defined, and stakeholders were identified.
- The potential effects on each stakeholder were discussed.
- A plan that might solve the crisis was proposed and discussed in detail.
- Stakeholders with a need-to-know were brought into the discussion; they added new intelligence.
- A plan was decided, agreements were reached, signed, and executed.

The key to it all was intelligence—actionable information.

The United States government's "Intelligence Community" presently includes eighteen federal agencies, each tasked with collecting specific types of information. US media reports suggest that hundreds of federal, state, and local agencies, plus private companies—hundreds of thousands of individuals—also contribute to the gathering. Similar communities exist in other countries.

Some of the threats that the world faces are obvious. As this book was being written, the Israel-Hamas conflict (which began on October 7, 2023) continues. The threat of escalation (expansion to other countries) was very real to anyone who watched the evening news. Other threats were present—terror plots and cybersecurity breaches—

which were essentially unknown outside the intelligence and law enforcement communities.

Like the example, these intelligence community members share and discuss the information gathered and how it should be acted upon. Plans are made and carried out, and if it all comes together in a "best-case" scenario, the other stakeholders—the general public—will never know that they happened.

The SWOT Analysis

Suppose you're not in crisis at the moment; are you safe? As mentioned, there's always a crisis somewhere; threats are universal and constant, and "good times" are times between crises, not the absence thereof. In looking toward your ultimate goal, the prevention of crises, a pre-crisis analysis of your current situation is a smart move. Enter the SWOT Analysis.

The SWOT Analysis—an acronym for **S**trengths, **W**eaknesses, **O**pportunities, and **T**hreats—can predict potential problems before they become crises. Once you've identified and assembled your strengths, weaknesses, opportunities, and threats, the SWOT matrix lays everything out in a clear, easy-to-read table. Managers can then see connections among the factors, such as: Does this strength support that opportunity? If we eliminate this weakness, would it create an additional opportunity for us? Are our strengths sufficient to overcome the threats we foresee? And so on.

SWOT sees both internal and external factors. Identifying strengths and weaknesses could be called an exercise in knowing yourself. Identifying opportunities and threats could be called an exercise in watching the world. Both are key elements of situational awareness. If reviewed regularly and incorporated into discussions of KPIs, tactical and strategic goals, and other business or personal processes, SWOT can assist leaders in developing strategies for most effectively using strengths to:

- Improve on strengths.
- Take advantage of opportunities.
- Address and overcome weaknesses.
- Minimize or eliminate threats.

For example, a small manufacturer's SWOT might look something like this:

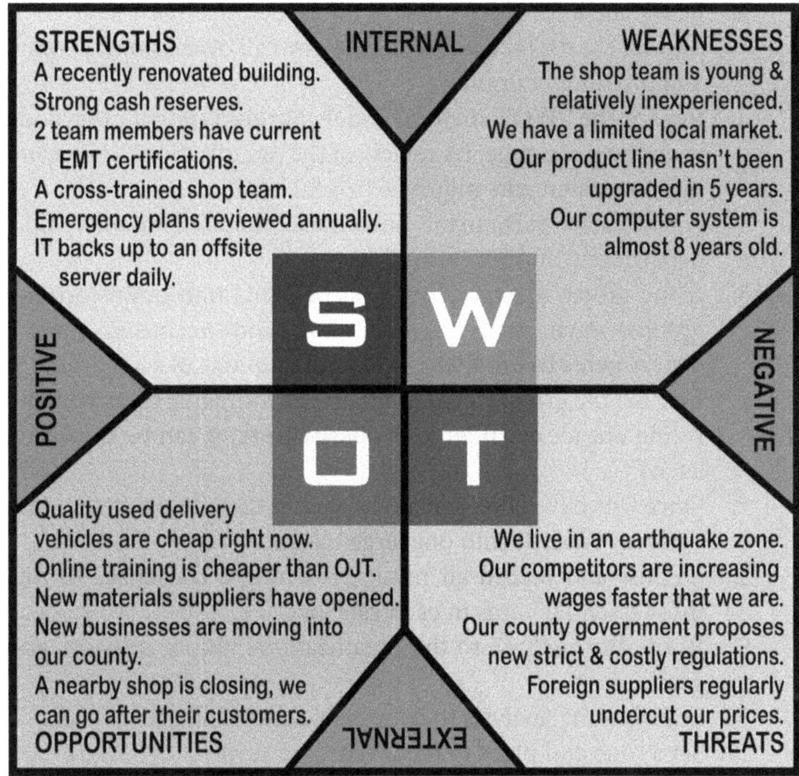

STRENGTHS
A recently renovated building.
Strong cash reserves.
2 team members have current EMT certifications.
A cross-trained shop team.
Emergency plans reviewed annually.
IT backs up to an offsite server daily.
INTERNAL
WEAKNESSES
The shop team is young & relatively inexperienced.
We have a limited local market.
Our product line hasn't been upgraded in 5 years.
Our computer system is almost 8 years old.
POSITIVE
S
W
O
T
NEGATIVE
Quality used delivery vehicles are cheap right now.
Online training is cheaper than OJT.
New materials suppliers have opened.
New businesses are moving into our county.
A nearby shop is closing, we can go after their customers.
OPPORTUNITIES
EXTERNAL
We live in an earthquake zone.
Our competitors are increasing wages faster that we are.
Our county government proposes new strict & costly regulations.
Foreign suppliers regularly undercut our prices.
THREATS

Understanding an organization's SWOT can also:

- Identify new opportunities or solutions to problems by demonstrating that strengths are not fully utilized.
- Assist in identifying where changes in priorities might be needed based on changes in strengths and weaknesses.
- Demonstrate that plans require adjustment when a new opportunity opens new paths to success while a new threat closes an existing path.

Conducting a SWOT analysis

1. Designate a facilitator who can keep discussions moving and on an effective path.
2. Designate a recorder to assist the leader; list discussion items on wall charts; take notes on or record all discussions; prepare and distribute minutes.
3. Review the SWOT method and its purpose so that everybody is on the same page. (A review of the organization's vision and mission statements might be helpful here.)
4. Have each participant introduce themself—name, title, department, and responsibilities.
5. If the group is large, divide participants into brainstorming groups—each with a facilitator and recorder—mixing departments to provide a variety of opinions in each group.
6. Instruct the groups to be thorough, encouraging them to avoid ruling out ideas. (If an idea doesn't work, it can be discarded later.)
7. Once lists have been generated, gather the group together and combine the lists into one large matrix.
8. Discuss and record all results, reaching a consensus on the most essential items in each category.
9. Relate the analysis to the organization's vision, mission, and goals.
10. Translate the analysis to courses of action and action plans.
11. Set a time and place to reconvene and review.

SWOT in Crisis

When a crisis strikes, your situation changes. What changes does it bring to each item in your SWOT Matrix? A swift reassessment provides intelligence that can guide changes in plans and priorities. Remember our example of QCo and its fasteners? Their supplier, SpecFast, closed their shop. QCo's fastener supply was a strength—they had a steady supply. It's now a weakness—they have exactly 30 days' supply, after which they stop production of everything that used them.

QCo had two items that were, if I may put it so, below the owners' pay grade—they were details the owner never needed to worry about. Those items are now the owner's highest priority: Obtaining all the fasteners they can and finding a new supplier. This is, intentionally, a simplified, obvious example. Still, in other, more complex situations, a SWOT analysis can put all the factors in front of everyone, forming part of the crisis communications process. Keeping every involved stakeholder "in the loop" can prevent a crisis escalation.

Chapter 4

Determine a Path to Success

The Plan

Crisis management planning involves two steps:

- Choose a "course of action" (COA).
- Design an "action plan" (AP).

The COA is a comprehensive overview that sets objectives, including alternatives and calculates risks against benefits.

The AP is the roadmap—a detailed plan or list of tasks required to bring the COA to completion.

The Ishikawa Diagram

Named for its creator, Kaoru Ishikawa, the Father of Japanese Quality, it's also known as a fishbone diagram, herringbone diagram, or cause-and-effect diagram. It explains all the potential causes of a situation and how they may have contributed to it. Valued as a comprehensive and comprehendible visualization of the relationships between cause and effect, fishbone diagrams are used in crisis and non-crisis situations.

It's particularly valuable when used in conjunction with the "5 Why?" method of intelligence gathering. When a situation is identified, you ask why. You may get more than one answer. For example:

We have a hydraulic leak in a press that forms car bumpers. The problem might be related to:

The Machine Itself
Measurements
Materials
Technique
Operator
Environment

Each of those possibilities may have several probable causes:

The Machine Itself
- Regular maintenance not performed as required
- Damage occurred that went unnoticed

Measurements
- Press was incorrectly calibrated

Materials
- The inner diameter of the bumper
  - Settings out of specification
  - The specifications were incorrect
- The outer diameter of the bumper
  - Settings out of specification
  - The specifications were incorrect
- The hydraulic fluid
  - Wrong fluid
  - Overfilled
  - Underfilled

Operator
- Lack of Training
- Improper materials fed into machine

Operator fatigue due to overwork
Operator negligence due to not paying attention

Environment
Contamination of hydraulic fluid
Shop lightning too low for proper visibility
Shop too cold for the operator's comfort

A simple situation may have many possible contributory causes, which create a list that's long and, frankly, hard to digest. The Ishikawa Diagram clusters all the factors in a concise, easy-to-read format with the problem at the head and the probable causes laid out like the bones, clearly and simply. The management team can then examine each potential in its turn, eliminating them if they were not contributors. Whatever is left, according to Sherlock Holmes and others, are the problems to be corrected.

Ishikawa goes both ways. In this example, a problem and its causes must be identified. In the following example, an objective is defined, and an Ishikawa Diagram could be a valuable tool in determining what obstacles might've blocked the objective and how to overcome them. (You might want to plot one out as an exercise. What might go wrong? Then, determine how to deal with each potential problem.)

A Military Example

We've invaded an enemy country, and our battalion has been ordered to move northward toward the capital city through a valley with an army base at the far end.

COA

Our course of action (defined in orders to the battalion commander) is what we're expected to accomplish:

Remove the base as a threat—

- Plan A: Take the base intact, capture the soldiers, and secure the base and supplies for our use.
- Plan B: Destroy the base, inflicting as many casualties and destroying as much materiel as possible.

AP

Our action plan then defines how we accomplish:

- The valley is narrow enough that two separate columns could support each other if necessary. The valley walls are heavily wooded foothills, but the valley floor is open farmland.
- A & B Companies will approach on the east side of the valley while C, D, E & F Companies on the west side, both columns using trails and dirt roads under cover of darkness.
- One hour before dawn, the east column will launch a diversionary attack at the main gate, attracting as much attention as possible.
- At that same hour, the west column will have approached the fences along the west side, maintaining cover, ready to infiltrate when the east column diversion begins.
- Each platoon in the west column has a designated building to secure. The Battalion Lead Platoon targets the base command center. Company First Platoons was tasked to take other key buildings—the armory, hospital, power plant, and motor pool. Other platoons to less critical structures, All to be secured with as little damage as possible.
- Prisoners to be collected in the base athletic field, and materiel is to be secure *in situ*.
- If resistance is severe, the Battalion Commander will issue a coded message to move to Plan B. Companies will expend all effort and ordnance necessary to inflict maximum damage, rendering the base useless to the enemy.

In commercial terms, let's return to the major customer who buys a significant amount of your products but decides not to renew their contract with you: The COA becomes "get customers to replace the loss of sales." The AP will include market research on the potential for switching production to other products, personal contacts to other existing customers for referrals, new contacts with potential customers, gathering OSINT on potential new customers (to see if the company would be a profitable client), and much more.

The business also needs a secondary objective. If the customer cannot be replaced in a timely manner, the company may have to scale back. That means preparing the employees for possible layoffs, talking to bankers about potential financial impacts, and answering many other questions.

Whatever the scenario, you then carry out your AP, step by step, to complete the COA, all the time watching—with the OODA Loop and other tools—in case you find a need to pivot. (Always remember the military maxim, "No battle plan ever survives first contact with the enemy.")

Risk Assessment

As part of COA-AP planning, I always include a risk assessment of an action plan prior to calling that plan final. The assessment can be quick—the time required depends on the complexity of the crisis but shouldn't require weeks or months because you often don't have that much time to get your plan into the field. That's where the MDMP comes in. Its greatest strength lies in its assumption that threats exist and you must be prepared with plans before the crisis develops. In life-or-death situations, you haven't time for a formal planning process—you do an immediate assessment and then act on instinct—meaning you have a plan and have practiced it. In other cases, the situation might be small enough that you can completely create the plan in your mind in a few minutes.

However, I never advise making it up as you go along. (That would put crisis consultants like me out of business, you know.) For example, a fire breaks out in a small manufacturing plant:

The first and greatest risk is to personnel, so you get on the intercom and shout, "Abandon ship! Abandon ship!" or some equivalent. A fire is an obvious and (sadly) all-too-common crisis. You should've designated gathering places for each team and drilled people. Hence, they know where to gather and tasked managers or supervisors with a roll call. You might also train a fire team to attack small blazes with the fire extinguishers you've strategically placed around your building.

The second priority is securing what we'll call "escalators"—volatile chemicals or other things that could worsen the situation. That may mean a team of employees trained to move the chemicals or secure fireproof doors as they exit. Before the fire, ask questions like: Are the storage areas clearly marked so firefighters can see them? Can the escalators be moved to another nearby structure? Simple, obvious questions that arise from your "measured paranoia."

The rest of the priorities may vary, depending on the nature of the business: Equipment that you need to produce your product or conduct business; the product you need to deliver to fulfill contracts and get paid so you can afford repairs; prototypes of potential new products; the list is long, and the priority rankings might be entirely subjective.

The point cannot be overstressed and, therefore, will be repeated for emphasis: In structuring a plan, like every other aspect of crisis management, intelligence is vital. You can't make your best decisions without the most complete and accurate information.

A secondary point is equally important and repeats: Since no crisis arises exactly according to plan, have a plan B or C or all the way down to Z if that's what it takes to cover the reasonably foreseeable possibilities.

Crisis Decision Frameworks: Adapting Decision-Making Processes

The Butterfly Effect

> No man is an island, Entire of itself;
> Every man is a piece of the continent, A part of the main.
>
> If a clod be washed away by the sea, Europe is the less,
> As well as if a promontory were:
> As well as if a manor of thy friend's or of thine own were.
>
> Any man's death diminishes me, Because I am involved in mankind.
> And therefore never send to know for whom the bell tolls; It tolls for thee.
>
> —John Donne[10]

[10] John Donne, *Devotions Upon Emergent Occasions, and severall steps in my Sicknes*, 1624. Read the full poem at https://allpoetry.com/No-man-is-an-island, accessed July 25, 2024 (and elsewhere).

I like this poem and the ideas we call "the butterfly effect" or "the law of unintended consequences." They remind us that we—individuals, companies, communities, nations—are connected, related, and interdependent. You've all heard one of these philosophies, and I'm sure you've also experienced its effects—anything that affects one affects all. Of course, like a sound wave, the effect lessens as we get father away from the incident.

Most of those effects are unnoticeable, like debiting or crediting a dollar to the ledger of a million-dollar-per-year business. Even so, those effects can be cumulative or predictive; eventually, something will happen that escapes one's notice!

Several methods have been developed to deal with future events. In my businesses, we use three:

The Military Decision-Making Process (MDMP)

In the military, we often hear, "No battle plan ever survives first contact with the enemy." In the Battle of Midway, in the early days of World War II, the Japanese battle plan was based on two crucial factors:

- Admiral William Halsey, a very bold fighter, would command the American defense forces.
- The attack would be a surprise similar to the attack on Pearl Harbor.

  Unfortunately, for the Japanese:
- Halsey got sick; therefore, Admiral Chester Nimitz relieved him of duty and sent him to hospital. To command the *Enterprise* battle group, Nimitz assigned Admiral Ray Spruance, a more cautious officer. Spruance moved more slowly than the Japanese expected Halsey to move. His command style altered the flow of the combat.
- The Allies had broken the Japanese code. Nimitz's intelligence officer, Commander Edwin Layton, knew a Japanese attack was coming and tricked the Japanese into revealing their target. When the Japanese Fleet arrived, the Americans were waiting.

Unable to quickly alter their battle plan, the Japanese suffered a massive defeat due to one ridiculously small and one very major change in the situation.

Stages

1. Receipt of Mission

The mission, threat, or crisis may come from anywhere, the worst being circumstances beyond the control of anyone involved in the group.

2. Mission Analysis

Gather and analyze intelligence; consider variables, options, and consequences; determine a "successful" outcome: The completion of the mission. The elimination or mitigation of the threat. The recovery from the crisis. Ask yourselves: What situation constitutes a "best-case scenario" improvement of the present situation?

3. Course of Action (COA) Development

Identify what actions you'll take—when, where, how, and why you'll take them. Give yourself several options whenever possible.

4. COA Analysis (aka Wargaming)

Test the plan, practice the actions under as-close-as-possible to the actual (anticipated) situation, and observe successes, failures, and consequences.

5. COA Comparison

Evaluate the practice outcomes compared to expectations. Choose the best option.

6. COA Approval

If the plan is created by lower echelons, agreement by upper echelons (owners, senior management, government agencies) may be required. Once obtained, create an action plan.

7. Orders Production

Orders are issued to all appropriate sub-units so they can prepare and conduct their actions within the COA.

Applying the MDMP to Non-Military Contexts

Scenario 15: The Family Farm

A small, family-owned farm decides to sell its honey directly to the public. A year later, several people went to the hospital. Tainted honey is reported as the cause. The farmers, realizing the threat to their livelihood, act quickly:

1. Receipt of Mission

Demonstrate that their product was not at fault or, if it was, that proper corrective actions are taken.

2. Mission Analysis

Possibility A: The farm was not at fault, but consumer confidence was damaged.

Possibility B: The farm was at fault, and the manufacturing process requires correction.

3. Course of Action (COA) Development

Outside experts are contracted to examine every aspect of the process, from the bee to the bottle. They are tasked to determine any points in the process where contamination could've occurred. Separately, products in stores are sequestered and randomly tested for product safety.

4. COA Analysis (aka Wargaming)

If this potential crisis had been envisioned, lawyers would've been consulted for liability issues. Engineers would've been consulted on potential process revisions. Independent laboratories would've been consulted regarding testing at the plant and in the stores. Accountants would've budgeted for testing the process and product, for recall and destruction if the product fails the tests, and for correcting the flawed processes.

5. COA Comparison

A few random jars were taken from each store and tested—results were negative. The collection and processing facilities were tested at each step—results were negative. Bees were tested for contamination—results negative. Conclusion: The so-called "tainted" honey was not tainted and was not the cause of the illnesses.

6. COA Approval

The farm owners reviewed the proposal and simulation and approved the plans at each step.

7. Orders Production

Having covered all the bases and achieved positive results, new standard operating procedures (SOPs) are written and distributed to all stakeholders to prevent a recurrence.

Conclusion

After action, reports are reviewed by the owners, lawyers, accountants, and others. These new SOPs will also be reviewed periodically and revised as needed. The farm continues operation with minimal damage to its profitability and an enhanced reputation among those who pay attention.

Positives

There is a clear chain of command. Operations are structured, with personnel knowing exactly their place and job expectations. It's well-tested through centuries of use and, in the modern age, is constantly being improved with new training and technology. It is designed for high-pressure situations where rapid changes and mind-boggling uncertainties are the norm. It recognizes the inherent uncertainties of every situation. During the preparation stages, there is a systematic appraisal and assessment of variables, what challenges they give rise to, and how to cope with changes. Every action concludes with the "after-action report" that evaluates the plan, the effectiveness of the plan, the consequences of the plan and assigns praise and blame, with awards and penalties as appropriate.

The MDMP is a solid crisis-management approach because the military is entirely a crisis-management organization.

Negatives

When an operation is too structured and very fluid, people may not be prepared to pivot to a new plan quickly enough. A tightly-structured management may discourage the free thinking and flexibility needed to meet some situations—the "that's not my job" excuse—or it might also encourage cutting corners and other misbehaviors—the "I was just following orders" excuse.

Variables for the military may include terrain, weather, intelligence, size and location of the opposing force, your arsenal, ammunition cache, the training your units have had, and the skills of the commanders. Some of these are controllable; others are not. All can influence the outcome of the battle.

As previously noted, intelligence (knowledge of the variables) is the prime variable. Time is the second most vital variable. Suppose (and this has happened) you encounter an unexpected enemy, like police finding a hostage situation in a building. Ideally, you should take time to evaluate this situation; however, with threats flying and tensions heightening by the second, a few minutes might be too late. The enemy is in control of the situation and ready to take lives. What do you do in a time-crunch situation? A strict military-style management style might not have the flexibility of mind to fall back on instinct and muscle memory. In this case, if they surprised you, you should return the favor to level the playing field.

In one such incident some years ago, the incident commander was able to call in a fighter plane to fly low and fast over a train where hostages were being held. The noise and jet wash (think waves from a speeding boat) so distracted the hostage-takers that law enforcement could move on them successfully. Of course, few people have access to a front-line fighter jet, so if you need a surprise, you may have to resort to something less surprising than a sonic boom 20 feet above you.

Order, control, and the need for preparation are proven valuable hallmarks of the MDMP. Still, sometimes, you need to be creative.

THE CARVER TECHNIQUE

The CARVER Technique is widely used in military, law enforcement, and security settings to evaluate targets to best allocate resources for potential attacks. CARVER stands for:

Criticality
Accessibility
Recuperability
Vulnerability
Effect
Recognizability

Criticality—the Importance of the Target

Critical targets are essential to the success of an operation or mission, such as a power plant or a communications center.

Accessibility—the Ease of Entry

Military bases are secure. They have walls, fences, guards carrying large, intimidating weapons, and every person on that base is trained to be on the lookout for people who don't appear to belong. A shopping mall is precisely the opposite; it encourages everybody to come in and freely enjoy its offerings.

Recuperability—Time to Recover

If you want to take out power in a neighborhood, you can take out one substation, or you can take out 200 telephone poles. The larger, more complex substation might be quicker to repair or replace than 200 smaller, simpler, widely separate locations. Those widely separate locations, however, will be far more difficult to destroy simultaneously.

Vulnerability—Internal Weaknesses or Flaws

An 80-year-old building in Salt Lake County, Utah, will be more vulnerable to an earthquake than a 25-year-old building because Utah wasn't known to be an earthquake zone 80 years ago. Those antique building codes didn't make provisions for the magnitude 5.9 quake that the County suffered in 2020, and it showed.

Effect—Impact of Target's Loss

Loss of life (a bomb explodes in a football stadium), loss of service (a bomb explodes at a powerplant), economic damage (A-bomb explodes inside the Fort Knox gold vault), loss of confidence or reputation (a bombshell story explodes all over the front pages), loss of data (a bomb explodes at a server farm), loss of mobility (an earthquake brings down several highway interchanges in a city), the list goes on.

Recognizability—Desirability as a Target

Facilities easily recognized as targets—government buildings, high-profile celebrities, key infrastructures—must be assumed to be on somebody's target list—or somewhere on everybody's.

Score: Good News—Bad News

By analyzing these six factors, professionals can better understand potential risks associated with specific locations or events. In CARVER, each component is assigned a score based on its relative importance to the adversary. These scores are then used to calculate a weighted total for the target, which can be used to prioritize targets based on their value to the adversary. Obviously, different adversaries and situations have different goals, so the CARVER score will differ based on circumstances.

The good news: CARVER intelligence can guide defense-mitigation strategies.

The bad news: CARVER is also used by the bad players to select potential targets and guide offense-destruction strategies.

To use the CARVER technique, each component is assigned a score based on its relative importance to the adversary. These scores are then used to calculate a weighted total score for the target, which can be used to prioritize targets based on their attractiveness to the adversary.

In today's rapidly evolving technological landscape, organizations face an ever-growing number of threats. These range from cyber-attacks to physical attacks, including natural disasters, industrial espionage, terrorism, supply chain disruptions, and even "treason" by trusted employees.

Examples of target analysis using the CARVER technique can include a financial institution analyzing the potential for a cyber-attack or infrastructure managers analyzing the potential for a physical attack. Best practices for a CARVER analysis include involving stakeholders from across the organization, incorporating threat modeling and risk assessment methodologies, and continuously reviewing and updating the analysis as the landscape evolves.

Prioritizing Targets

There's an old saying, "Nothing is foolproof because fools are so damn clever." It's equally true that nothing can be perfectly secure because of the costs, the inconveniences imposed by security, and the fact that adversaries are constantly devising new strategies to make honest peoples' lives more difficult. Therefore, priorities must be set, and effective security management includes more than identifying targets. Organizations must carefully allocate resources with a focus on their most critical assets.

The CARVER Technique sets priorities as objectively as possible, but organizations may factor in other considerations depending on their own goals.

For example, a political party prioritizes winning elections over all other factors because they have no power if they don't win. The political leaders and large donors often have and, undoubtedly, will continue to protect candidates they consider more likely winners while refusing support to those with lower poll numbers. The best candidate to serve the people's needs becomes a secondary priority—if it ever was a priority.

For any business, profitability is its highest priority. Many, therefore, choose to quietly pay off ransomware attacks rather than risk loss of critical data, just as parents might decide to quietly pay a kidnapper's demands rather than trust law enforcement to recover their child.

These are never the best choices, but an old joke reminds us, "Sometimes corporate boards make decisions no five-year-old would approve of. Sadly, there's never a five-year-old in a boardroom when you need one."

Best Practices

CARVER analyses are most accurate and effective when they involve stakeholders across the organization. An outside risk management firm is also an option, but that, too, has positives and negatives: They may be more objective than an in-house team. They will never understand your needs and priorities as well as you do.

Either way, ensure (as best you can) that all perspectives are considered. General threat modeling and risk assessment methodologies should also be part of CARVER analyses to provide a more comprehensive view of potential threats and vulnerabilities. Above all other factors, reviewing and updating the analyses regularly is essential to reflect changes in the threat landscape and the organization's priorities.

Real-World Scenarios

The US military uses CARVER to identify potential targets during military operations. It has been proven in numerous campaigns, including the recent Gulf War, where it was used to identify and prioritize targets for air strikes.

This chart is a real example of a military application. In this scenario, the possible targets are staged from one to five. The attributes to prioritize targets are allocated to the staging. In the example, five sample resources are evaluated with the CARVER score. In the column "targets," we have five examples of possible targets the adversary could attack.

Table 1A

The least significant factor is listed as rank one (1), while the most is marked five (5). The rows with the highest CARVER rankings, the Command Post and Staging Area, will most likely be attacked. To counter these potential attacks, several options are available:

- Lower accessibility with additional security layers, entrance checks, and barriers.
- Increase recoverability by training a successor to each leader.
- Move the successors to separate locations.
- Move the command post to an underground facility to decrease visibility and increase stealth.

Targets	C	A	R	V	E	R	Overall Rank
Command Post	5	2	5	3	4	5	24
Feeding Point	4	3	3	3	3	2	18
Military Camp	3	4	1	3	2	5	18
Staging Area	2	5	1	5	2	5	20
Weapons Cache	4	5	3	2	2	1	17

Table 1B

If the analysts prefer, descriptives can replace numbers:

Targets	C	A	R	V	E	R
Command Post	Loss would cause total failure	Extremely difficult to Access	Extremely difficult to replace	No direct attack capability	Critical loss of life & resources	Easily recognized by all
Feeding Point	Loss would reduce performance	Not difficult to access	Replaceable in a short period of time	Severe direct attack capability	High loss of life; low loss of resources	Recognized with training
Military Camp	Loss would reduce capabilities considerable	Very difficult to access	Difficult to replace	Severe direct attack capability	Low loss of life & resources	Easily recognized by all

Targets	C	A	R	V	E	R
Staging Area	Loss may reduce performance	Not difficult to access	Easily replaced quickly	Little direct attack capability	Little loss of life or resources	Hard to recognize
Weapons Cache	Loss would have no effect	Extremely difficult to access	Immediately replaceable with no down time	No direct attack capability	Low loss of life; high loss of resources	Extremely difficult to recognize

Table 2

The ranking system can also be applied in a broad business context by replacing "targets" with departments, facilities, products, processes, or any other business factor. For a business, the table might look like this:

Department	C	A	R	V	E	R	Overall Rank
Finance	4	3	3	3	3	2	18
HR	4	5	3	2	2	1	17
Operations	3	4	1	3	2	5	18
Purchasing	2	5	1	5	2	5	20
Quality	5	2	5	3	4	5	24

Positives

CARVER's simplicity and adaptability make it useful in almost any situation. It's a straightforward and intuitive scoring system that requires no complex tools. It promotes a consistent framework that aids resource allocation.

It blends qualitative and quantitative assessments. The rankings are always, to a degree, qualitative (opinion-based), but once the individual rankings are agreed on, the final rankings become quantitative and are not subject to debate. The CARVER Technique can streamline the decision-making process.

Negatives

CARVER focuses primarily on the attractiveness of targets to the adversary rather than considering the defender's perspective. This can result in a narrow view of the potential threats and vulnerabilities, leading to ineffective or incomplete risk management strategies.

The Technique is based on a static analysis of potential targets, which may not reflect the dynamic nature of the threat landscape. Where threat landscapes are constantly evolving, target priorities must also change rapidly.

Threat modeling and risk assessment should provide a fairly comprehensive view of potential vulnerabilities. Analyses should be reviewed and updated regularly to reflect known changes in the threat landscape and organizational priorities.

Enhancing the analysis by involving stakeholders representing all segments of the organization and a team approach can provide a more comprehensive view of threats and vulnerabilities, ensuring the best analysis possible.

The OODA Loop

Short for "Observe, Orient, Decide, Act," it's called a loop to underscore the continuous nature of decision-making in dynamic, competitive environments. I find it most useful for competitive environments. It promotes rapid responses that are processed in real time. It compares real-time info with known variables. Using the loop, one decides a course and then does it, repeated as necessary.

1. Observe

Crisis managers continuously watch for changes in their situation, gaining situational awareness via all senses. These observations may come from many paths, including, in complex situations, observations on the group's internal status.

2. Orient

Contextualize what you observe based on everything you know. The individual decision-makers should generally do the orienting. Still, organizations can design their internal systems to enhance decision-makers' freedom.

3. Decide

Formulate a best-guess course of action. Decisions are more complicated in this version: Some must be made almost instantaneously, based on the situation. In such cases, observation leads directly to action.

4. Act

Execute your decision without delay.[11]

Positives

The OODA Loop is effective because it allows you to deal with fast-changing scenarios. You can deal with multiple unrelated problems that are arising, some of which might be, as we've named them, "manufactured crises" by the press (more on that later) or by unions (wanting a better contract).

In family financial planning, for example, a diverse portfolio gives you options: If stocks drop, take money out of the market and buy precious metals or municipal bonds. If precious metals are rising, sell some and use the cash to buy some stocks your research says are undervalued. In particular:

- Leadership must devolve to lower levels.
- Provides real flexibility in real time
- Can deal with multiple situations simultaneously

[11] Adapted from Unbylined, "The OODA Loop Explained: The real story about the ultimate model for decision-making in competitive environments," *OODAloop.com*. Reston, VA: OODA LLC, 2023. https://www.oodaloop.com/the-ooda-loop-explained-the-real-story-about-the-ultimate-model-for-decision-making-in-competitive-environments/, accessed July 25, 2024.

- Quick actions make countermeasures difficult.

Negatives

OODA Loop operates entirely on tactics. Some say that winning, in war, commerce, or elsewhere, is the total of all the tactical actions. Tactics, however, don't add up to a strategy.

Take law enforcement as an example. Catching criminals in a neighborhood with rising crime rates doesn't reduce crime; there's always someone waiting to take a neighborhood kingpin's place. Determining the root or ultimate cause of the criminal activity—lack of money, job opportunities, and so on—and providing viable alternatives for a better life has a far superior chance of major, long-term change in that neighborhood. In particular:

- Operates only on a tactical level
- Cannot act when permissions are required
- Can be overwhelmed by evolving situations
- Demands top-tier situational awareness

The Attack Tree Analysis (ATA)

The Attack Tree Analysis (ATA) can aid any of these methods by providing additional insights into vulnerabilities and assisting countermeasures development by breaking down potential attack scenarios into manageable components.

ATA takes a top-down approach, starting with identifying high-level goals an attacker might have and then breaking them down into lower-level sub-goals and attack paths. This visual representation provides a comprehensive overview of potential vulnerabilities, attack vectors, and countermeasures:

Components

1. The Root Node represents the main objective of an attacker, such as extracting sensitive information. It serves as the starting point for the analysis and branches out into various attack paths.

2. Attack Paths represent the separate ways an attacker can achieve their objective. Each path is further divided into subgoals until the lowest level of attack steps is reached.
3. Leaf Nodes represent the lowest-level attack steps or vulnerabilities. These typically include specific actions an attacker can take, such as exploiting software vulnerabilities or conducting social engineering attacks.
4. Countermeasures mitigate the risks identified in the tree. Specific countermeasures are assigned to specific nodes in the tree to clarify the effectiveness of existing security measures or identify gaps that need to be addressed.

Significance

1. Comprehensive Risk Assessment, a structured approach to understanding potential attack vectors and vulnerabilities and assisting in developing comprehensive assessment and mitigation efforts.
2. Proactive Defense Planning enables organizations to proactively defend by visualizing attack paths, identifying weak points, and preparing defense alternatives.
3. Resource Allocation Optimization through the identification of critical areas.
4. Compliance with regulatory requirements goes more smoothly when thorough risk assessments have been completed and appropriate countermeasures are in place.

Applying the Technique to Emerging Threats

Some threats are envisioned but not yet fully understood or realized—the Internet of Things (IoT) and artificial intelligence (AI). It takes a little imagination, but an ATA can identify potential targets for these emerging threats based on past experience.

For example, the IoT might still connect devices and sensors that are not now utilizing the Web. CARVER can identify theoretical possibilities based on the same criteria as existing threats. Organizations can then develop effective security measures against threats, which we hope will never actually exist.

Scenario Planning: Preparing for Multiple Outcomes

Let's look at an extreme example: A special forces team is tasked to rescue hostages from some fortified enemy location. Command decides to do it at night because you have the advantages of night vision and other technologies the enemy doesn't possess. These low-level terrorists assume a rescue attempt will be made, so mission success depends on surprise, stealth, terrain, and other factors—surprise being the most vital.

1. Observation

Gathering intelligence on the enemy's number; the types of weapons and ammunition stockpile; the vehicles and petrol supply; where in the compound the hostages are being held; do they have canine or human sentries; do they have booby traps, IADs, or the like; the compound's location and proximity of support (for the terrorists and the rescue team), and anything other intelligence they can gather. This is the observation phase.

2. Orientation

The team synthesizes this intelligence and compares the situation to their capability. Do I have snipers available; do I have drones or night vision goggles to observe; how much time until the anticipated rendezvous with the extraction team; what other skills do I have on my team that I can bring to bear on the enemy; what experience do I have with my team in similar situations. As this process goes on, I connect with external factors like weather and environment.

3. Decision

Based on my orientation, I insert my A-team using a helicopter on the (sloping) roof, while the B-team goes under cover of darkness over the wall around the compound.

4. Action

We execute the plan, and while executing, we keep our eyes and ears open for a changing situation. In this case, there are small booby traps that could only be seen up close if you were paying close attention. We can't, therefore, go straight in; we take a longer, more circuitous-but-safer route and meet up with the A-team after they're inside the main building. Here, we find barricaded doors and snipers requiring additional modifications to the plan.

There are no surprises, and we rescue the hostages without loss of life among those we care about. We arrive at the extraction point, and everybody lives happily ever after, except the terrorists, among whom there were no survivors.

In the civilian world, let us say a new car with hands-free driving and the "driver" falls asleep. This car crashed into a white wall because the sensors did not detect a white wall or didn't recognize the white wall as a wall. You may choose to deal with this situation via MDMP because you have time to do so. Then you receive reports from another car crash in California and the same from Texas and Florida. Now, you must move quickly because this incident isn't isolated. You can see a sequence. You no longer have much time, so you may switch to an OODA Loop decision process.

While writing this book, several computer network problems were reported in the news. First, car dealerships across the USA had their parts and warehousing servers go down. This was only an inconvenience; the dealerships moved to paper and pencil order processing. Within weeks, however, banks and airlines reported similar problems. They cannot simply go to paper; they're no longer set up for that situation. This is more serious because workers and families are now affected. Does my credit/debit card work? Do I have cash on hand to pay for my food? Am I stranded 1,000 miles from home? Can I rent a car or take a train, or are there no viable travel options available?

As the news reports come in, you know your company depends on cyberspace to operate. You now must be thinking, "Is my industry next?" You engage the CARVER method to determine how vulnerable you are to attack, where it might originate, and how to combat it.

Conclusion

The MDMP focuses on pre-planning for situations. "This is what we expect to happen. This is what we think might happen. Therefore, these are the various strategies that we may use depending on what we see when we get there."

The CARVER Technique focuses on targets and setting priorities for defending those targets from potential attacks. "This is our desired outcome in this situation, which is our desire for that situation. Therefore, these are the various strategies that we may use to arrive at those ends."

An ATA reminds us that vulnerabilities may be exploited from various avenues and assists in countermeasures development using a top-down approach, from the identification of high-level goals to low-level sub-goals and attack paths. "This is happening; therefore, this is how we must respond to achieve our goals."

The OODA Loop focuses on the moment of action. We've trained for various situations but don't choose our tactics until we get to the scene and see the details. Then, we pick from a group of scenarios exactly how we will attack a problem. "This is how the situation has changed; therefore, we adjust our plan thus and thus."

Any of these decision-making methods can and should be wargamed. By designing scenarios and altering parameters—the nature of the crisis, locations, number of people involved, weather—virtually any variable, plans can be made to meet a variety of potential threats. Your people can gain critical thinking skills, increase their situational awareness, develop flexible attitudes, and better understand the unpredictable nature of life, especially in crises.

One Final Thought

Technology has provided us with magnificent tools, but they have limitations. Humans are the ultimate technology, but we have limitations. None of those need to be detailed here; the press generally publicizes failures as fast or faster than they publish successes. I want to mention a significant failure of each:

- For years, the Israel-Gaza border was saturated with intelligence-gathering technology. In the hours leading up to the October 2023 attacks, Hamas acquired drones and flew them kamikaze-like into cameras and other equipment, destroying the technology. Had military personnel—literally, a few men in towers with binoculars and radios—been on guard, one of them would've seen the attack coming. They, too, would've been targeted for elimination. Still, it would have taken only one to relay a message to a command post, potentially changing the outcome of that day.
- In the late 1960s and early 1970s, Israeli intelligence tapped into ("bugged") the Cairo phone system. Prior to the 1973 Yom Kippur War, Israeli leaders were expecting this "special means of collection," as they called it back then, to warn them of an impending attack. Someone, however, neglected to activate the system during the vital days before the Arab attack. As a result, it wasn't collecting the vital intelligence when it was most needed.

That final thought is, "No system is perfect."

Chapter 5

Manage the Problem, Not the Symptoms

"Don't Just stand There, Do Something!"

If you watch a lot of movies, you'll hear that phrase often. It's a Hollywood cliché that excites the audience and increases their anticipation for what the hero is about to do. While great for Hollywood, this attitude is not always successful in businesses, governments, or homes.

In every situation, you do need to do ***some***-thing, but that needs to be the ***right*** thing, and it needs to be done at ***the right time***. If you have a plan, you need to carry out that plan; If you don't have a plan, you need to do those things I discussed in Chapter 4. You may need to do them quickly, not worrying about doing them perfectly, then carry out the best plan you can develop in whatever time you have. In a crisis, the ***tactical mindset*** will be your most valuable ally.

The Tactical Mindset

In some situations, split-second choices can mean the difference between life and death. For business owners, that's not common, but making timely and well-informed choices is. Decision-making under duress can ensure personal safety and well-being in everyday personal situations.

Think about the professionals in high-risk jobs, such as paramedics, pilots, and firefighters. They have well-defined procedures and checklists that act like a carefully choreographed dance. These procedures ensure the best chance of successful outcomes. Well, you might recall (from a few years ago) several incidents of ambushes against first responders.[12] That wasn't in their playbook; it hadn't happened before. Those first responders had to make up a completely new dance at that moment.

These scenarios are aptly termed "absence of procedure." It's a gray zone where no step-by-step system exists. On such days, professionals have extensive training; many have years of experience, which combine to create mental "muscle memory"—good instincts for dealing with the unexpected. The rest of us have only our natural instincts and intuition. Either way, the circumstances never solve themselves; we must deal with the tactical (immediate) situation the best we can.

The Role of the Tactical Mindset

The tactical mindset enables you to make quick, effective decisions:

- It blends analytical skills and an intuitive grasp of the situation.
- It requires you to understand the situation logically while being mindful of (but not controlled by) your emotions in that situation.
- It involves seeing the big picture while understanding finer details, foreseeing potential obstacles, and skillfully navigating a path forward.

[12] For example, see, Josh Campbell, "US Counterterrorism Officials Warn Police to be on Alert for Ambush Attacks," *CNN.com*. Atlanta: Cable News Network, January 17, 2020. https://www.cnn.com/2020/01/15/politics/us-counterterrorism-officials-warn-police-to-be-on-alert-for-ambush-attacks/index.html, accessed September 19, 2024.

Cultivating the Tactical Mindset

There's no difference between developing a tactical mindset and mastering any other skill. It simply requires repeated training and repeated practice. Engaging in simulations, role-playing, or real-life scenarios can challenge your decision-making abilities and sharpen your skills. The dynamic nature of the world means that continuous learning is essential.

Staying updated through reading, attending workshops, networking, and on-the-job mentoring ensures you remain prepared for ever-evolving challenges. Attention-to-detail on the job and meditation off the job play crucial roles in this development. These practices enhance situational awareness and focus; they help you understand and manage internal biases and emotions that might cloud your judgment.

Surround yourself with mentors, peers, and subordinates who can provide candid feedback on decisions and offer valuable insights. These outside perspectives help identify and fill in blind spots, further enhancing your skill.

The SWOT and OODA Loop techniques mentioned in Chapter 4 are tools to help you make decisions under pressure. Reviewing SWOT tells you where you're strong and where you need to improve. Employing OODA forces us to stop and think—to ask vital questions, including:

- Have we planned for something like this?
- Is this the full crisis, or is it a developing situation?
- Is this the problem, or are we looking at a symptom?

Finally, keep in mind the counsel of the college basketball coach who won seven consecutive NCAA championships:

> Never mistake activity for accomplishment.
>
> —John Wooden[13]

[13] John Wooden, quoted in Craig Impelman, "Never Mistake Activity for Achievement," *TheWoodenEffect.com*. Dallas: Success Partners LP, June 20, 2018. https://www.thewoodeneffect.com/activity-achievement/, accessed September 18, 2024.

Historical Examples

Throughout history, decision-making under duress has altered the course of events in ways both grand and subtle. Whether on the battlefield, in boardrooms, or during social upheavals, leaders have faced moments where quick and effective decisions have been the fulcrum on which destiny pivots:

Scenario 16: The 300 Spartans, 480 BC

During the Greco-Persian War, Persian emperor Xerxes invaded Greece with infantry and a fleet. The Spartan King Leonidas and 300 of his warriors led an estimated 7,000 Greeks from other city-states against a Persian force estimated at somewhere between 70,000 and 300,000. Vastly outnumbered, Leonidas established his Spartans in a mountain pass called Thermopylae. Defending a pass just a few yards wide as the other Greeks guarded his flanks and rear, Leonidas neutralized Xerxes' advantage. The Greeks were betrayed, but Leonidas refused to surrender. Their stand failed to stop the Persian advance. Still, they delayed him long enough for the Athenian navy to defeat the Persian fleet, a vital part of Xerxes' plan. The courageous stand of the Spartans became a rallying point for Greek unity and resistance. Xerxes' defeat influenced the course of Western civilization to the present day.

Scenario 17: The Battle of Gettysburg, 1863

General Robert Lee, who had been commanding the Confederate States Army for two years, seemed invincible. To force US President Abraham Lincoln into peace talks, Lee invaded Pennsylvania, hoping to draw the main force of the United States Army into a decisive defeat. When advance units of Union General George Meade discovered Lee's forces, they engaged. Though neither army was prepared for a battle, Meade saw that his forces held the high ground. Recognizing his strategic advantage, Meade ordered the Army to stand firm, forcing the Confederates to attack him. Over three days, Union commanders repelled Confederate advances, including the famous clash at Little Round Top and the devastating failure of Pickett's Charge. Combined with a victory that same day—by Union General Ulysses S. Grant at Vicksburg, Mississippi—the tide turned against the Confederacy, and Lee surrendered in April 1865.

Scenario 18: Rosa Parks Refuses to Yield Her Seat, 1955

Though slavery had been outlawed for almost a century, African-Americans had not yet achieved the promised equality. "Jim Crow" laws in many US states forced African-Americans into a segregated existence, including sitting in "Blacks Only" sections of public buses. On a wintry evening in Montgomery, Alabama, Rosa Parks sat on a bus in a front-row seat. When a European-American demanded she give him her seat, the woman, physically tired from a long day of work and fed up with how her people were treated, refused. Her decision led to her arrest, which ignited the Montgomery Bus Boycott, a pivotal moment in the Civil Rights Movement. Her act of defiance, driven by a quick decision under societal pressure, altered American society.

Scenario 19: The Cuban Missile Crisis, 1962

At the height of Cold War tensions between the United States and the Soviet Union, US spy planes discovered Soviet atomic missiles in Cuba. Having fought two wars in as many decades and with the new threat of Soviet atomic weapons, President John Kennedy faced immense pressure. Military commanders called for invasion, while diplomats called for a negotiated resolution. Knowing both courses held serious risks, Kennedy opted for a naval blockade of the island and back-channel negotiations directly with Soviet Premier Nikita Khrushchev. Kennedy's choice, actions, and the fact that he acted in secrecy that lacked politically valuable headlines prevented an atomic war. It highlighted the profound importance of calm deliberation amidst global duress.

Scenario 20: Apollo 13, 1970

When an oxygen tank exploded on Apollo 13, the mission to land on the moon turned into a fight for survival. NASA's flight director, Gene Kranz, and his team made rapid decisions under immense pressure—including the heat of public opinion as the world watched the rescue efforts. One key to the astronauts' survival was scrubbing carbon dioxide out of the life support system after the loss of the O_2 tank. The altered mission taxed the lunar module's scrubber system, so Earth-bound engineers literally had to connect a square peg (the command module O_2 filters) into a round hole (the lunar module O_2 scrubber) using only the equipment aboard the spacecraft. Improvising solutions to problems they had never been trained to solve, Kranz's team safely returned the astronauts to Earth. It highlighted the power of quick, collaborative problem-solving under duress.

Scenario 21: The Raid on Entebbe, 1976

When an Air France plane was highjacked to Entebbe, Uganda, Israeli Prime Minister Yitzhak Rabin faced a critical decision. Israel had a strict policy of never negotiating with terrorists, and Ugandan President Idi Amin deployed Ugandan soldiers to safeguard the terrorists. About half the hostages were released, but 106 remained—Israeli citizens and the flight crew. Rabin chose to launch a high-risk rescue operation. Israeli commandos flew under cover of darkness to Uganda, attacked the defenders, and rescued all but four hostages—three killed in the raid and another who was in a Ugandan hospital. (She was later murdered on Amin's orders.) Only one commando died. "Operation Entebbe" demonstrated the impact of decisive, courageous action under the worst possible conditions. (By the way, the operation was renamed "Operation Jonathan" after the commando leader who died. Jonathan Netanyahu was the brother of the current prime minister of Israel, Benjamin Netanyahu, who also served in the prestigious and highly secretive unit Sayaret Matkal in his younger days.)

Scenario 22: The Hudson Landing, 2009

As Captain Chesley "Sully" Sullenberger piloted his Airbus A320 away from New York City's LaGuardia Airport, his expected smooth flight almost became an epic tragedy. The plane ran through a flock of geese, damaging both engines. Sully and copilot Jeffrey Skiles had three nearby airports, but the plane was only half a mile above the ground when the geese hit. With seconds to decide, they determined that their crippled plane was too low to glide unpowered to any runway. Opting for a water landing, they brought the crippled airliner to a relatively smooth landing on the Hudson River near Manhattan island. US Coast Guard vessels and municipal ferries rescued the passengers and crew. Sully's extensive training and experience enabled him to make true split-second decisions that saved the 155 passengers and crew members.

Conclusion

Few of us will face such drastic circumstances, but these events underscore the importance of decisive action under duress. From battlefields to boardrooms, from skies to city streets, history's course has been altered by those who made fast choices when faced with overwhelming odds. They serve as both inspiration and lessons for all, highlighting the undeniable value of moving from panic to plan.

Preparation Is the Key Element of a Tactical Mindset

The tactical mindset begins with situational awareness. By staying attuned to your environment and yourself, you can detect changes, identify threats, and seize opportunities, enabling a proactive rather than reactive approach.

Those who embody this mindset employ diligent preparation. This isn't just about planning for known scenarios; it's about cultivating the mental flexibility to handle unforeseen challenges. The aim is not to predict every possible outcome but to develop the resilience and adaptability needed to tackle whatever situation arises.

When it comes to execution, a tactical mindset prioritizes agility over speed. With a solid foundation of awareness and preparation, we become able to change course when the unexpected arises or better opportunities emerge.

Finally, a tactical mindset emphasizes the importance of the after-action report. Even if the only person you report to is yourself, the decision has been made, and the plan has been executed. Serious introspection helps you understand what worked well, what could have been improved, and how to enhance your approach for future scenarios. This creates a cycle of preparing, acting, reflecting, learning, and growth.

The Cost of Indecision

> Lack of decision plus time is a decision.
>
> —Old Business Proverb

One obvious cost of indecision is the loss of opportunities. While we stand at the crossroads, pondering our options, time doesn't wait.

Opportunities to act, change, or make a positive impact can slip through our fingers. By failing to decide, we unintentionally choose the *status quo*.

Over the long term, indecision becomes stagnation. Regularly avoiding decisions keeps us in our comfort zones, stifles personal and professional growth, and prevents us from reaping potential rewards that always come with a little risk. Habitual hesitancy erodes our confidence. Each time we sidestep a decision due to fear or doubt, we send ourselves a subconscious message: "I can't handle this." Over time, this lie becomes true—you can't decide because you lack all confidence in your ability to make a good one. When the moment goes south, we stand like the deer in the headlights—frozen, unable to move—and end up as roadkill.

Every decision, or lack thereof, creates ripples in our lives. Indecision can lead to a series of unintended consequences, each stemming from our initial inaction. This ripple effect can compound the initial costs, leading to more complex situations down the line.

While fear of making the wrong choice is valid, we must understand that making no choice is often the worst decision. Every decision has a timer running. Eventually, the timer runs out, and the situation changes. We all know that we rarely, if ever, have total control over a given situation. If you fail to make any decision at all, you can't control the outcome at all.

The Psychology and Biology of Stress

At the heart of the human stress response is the ***amygdala***, an almond-shaped set of neurons deep in the brain's medial-temporal lobe. The amygdala as our rapid response unit, alerting us to immediate threats. When it perceives danger, it sends a distress signal to the hypothalamus, the brain's command center, which then activates the sympathetic nervous system, releasing a surge of adrenaline into the bloodstream.

We all know stress. It's the racing heartbeat before an important presentation, the cold sweat when facing an unforeseen obstacle, or the chest tightening in life-threatening situations. How do these physiological and psychological effects influence our capacity to make decisions?

Briefly, this adrenaline rush heightens our senses, preparing our bodies for the classic "fight or flight" response. In controlled bursts, this response is positive; it sharpens reflexes, focuses attention, and mobilizes energy reserves. Unfortunately, people lacking the tactical mindset don't fight or fly—they freeze. The fight or flight response is delayed. The freeze response is also normal and common in humans. The power of the tactical mindset lies in keeping the freeze time as brief as possible.

The Dangers

Under intense stress, people often experience "cognitive tunnelling"—the narrowing of our attention. We focus on the immediate threat to the exclusion of almost everything else. This is a valuable part of the tactical mindset, but cognitive tunnelling limits our ability to see the broader picture, evaluate long-term alternatives, or think creatively. Like the OODA Loop, it only works on a short-term tactical level.

If a perceived threat becomes overwhelming, cognitive tunneling becomes so narrow that we can't see the light at the end of the tunnel. Like the deer, we become paralyzed. That's the "I'm dead, let's get it over with" response. In most cases, that's a false conclusion; we are simply too shocked to respond correctly.

Duress can also cause what psychologist Daniel Goleman terms an "emotional highjack."[14] When our emotions overpower our logic, impulsive decisions follow with no thought of consequences. Imagine trying to steer a car when someone else has their foot on the accelerator. In such a situation, your driving is never your best.

As important as the tactical mindset is, over the long run, chronic exposure to stress hormones can hamper cognitive functions, affecting memory, attention, decision-making, and blood pressure, among other things. Chronic stress also has tangible physical impacts. It can disturb sleep, create muscle tension, and provoke headaches and digestive problems. Physical discomfort further impairs cognitive function, making decision-making even more challenging.

---

[14] Daniel Goleman, *Emotional Intelligence: Why It Can Matter More than IQ*. New York City: Random House Publishing Group, 1995.

Understanding the profound influence of stress on our tactical mindset helps us master our reactions. Be ready to act when needed, but learn to relax after the situation relaxes.

Historical Examples

Scenario 23: The United States Declines to Outlaw Slavery, 1776

Calls for the end of slavery in America came forcefully in 1776 during debates over the Declaration of Independence, but the southern states refused to agree. By 1787, as the Federal Convention debated the US Constitution, slavery had become integral to the southern economy. To ensure the adoption of those documents by slave-holding states, compromises allowing slavery to continue were included. In 1820, the Missouri Compromise limited the admission of new slave states. In 1850, the California Compromise allowed certain territories to choose to allow or outlaw slavery. In 1854, the Republican Party organized with a platform including the complete end of slavery in America. After 90 years of debate, the 1860 election of Abraham Lincoln pushed the southern states to secede, leading to the Civil War. Slavery was finally outlawed by the 13th Amendment on December 6, 1865. The costs of "kicking the decision down the road," as modern American politicians call it, were thousands of deaths, billions of dollars wasted, and millions of lives enslaved.

Scenario 24: Tsar Nicholas Refuses to Dismiss Rasputin, 1914

Tsar Nicholas II and Tsarina Alexandra had a son, Alexei, with hemophilia. Every injury was life-threatening and horrifyingly painful. A monk, Grigori Rasputin, convinced them he could alleviate the child's pain. Apparently successful, he became a significant influence in the Russian court. Despite reports of Rasputin's ungodly character, the couple refused to dismiss the charlatan. When World War I commenced, they followed Rasputin's advice over that of experienced soldiers and statesmen. His suggestions brought disaster, including leaving Alexandra in charge of the government while Nicholas took command of the

Army. Neither was qualified for those roles. Rasputin remained their principle advisor, despite mounting calls for his removal. With the War all but lost and the empire in disarray, the royal couple still hesitated to do what was needed. The solution came when Rasputin was murdered, and the Tsar was forced to abdicate, leading to the establishment of the communist-run Union of Soviet Socialist Republics.

Scenario 25: Kodak Creates Digital Cameras, 1975

Throughout most of the 20th Century, Kodak was synonymous with film photography and invented the digital camera in 1975. Worried that the new technology would hurt their film sales, they hesitated to bring it to market. Sony, meanwhile, demonstrated the first no-film camera in 1981, and Fujifilm introduced the first fully digital camera in 1988. Kodak didn't start selling digital cameras until 1995, when numerous other companies were major competitors. Kodak ended film sales in 2009 and film processing in 2012, the year they filed for bankruptcy. Once the premier company in its field, it's limited to a small specialty market.

By the way, some years later, Nokia became the world-leader in the cellphone industry. They also failed to explore and market new technologies. When Apple launched the iPhone, Nokia was unable to respond and lost most of its market share. The "Nokia effect" has since become a well-known business term for marketing hesitation.

The Eisenhower Matrix

The time a situation allots you will determine how much intelligence you can gather, affecting your options. Some situations, such as the mall shooter, require no intelligence gathering; the problem is clear and the response obvious. Other situations develop slowly, giving people time to gather the right intelligence, which dramatically increases your chances of arriving at the right solution. For many years, a tool has been in place to assist in determining how to handle various situations. However, this tool has limits.

	URGENT	NOT URGENT
IMPORTANT	**1:** Do These First **Time Critical:** Overdue or Due Now **Value:** Adds to Short-term Goals **Your Attention:** Required	**2:** Do These Soon **Time Sensitive:** Due Soon or Later **Value:** Adds to Long-Term Goals **Your Attention:** Required
NOT IMPORTANT	**3:** Delegate These **Time:** Overdue or Due Now **Value:** Adds Some **Your Attention:** Useful	**4:** Do These When Convenient **Not Time Sensitive:** Due Whenever **Value:** Adds Little **Your Attention:** Not Required

In a 1954 speech, Pres. Dwight Eisenhower presented a hypothesis by quoting an unnamed university president who said, "I have two kinds of problems, the urgent and the important. The urgent are not important, and the important are never urgent."[15] The theory has been codified as The Eisenhower Matrix and has gained wide use as a management tool.[16] It divides tasks into four ways:

Benefits of the Eisenhower Matrix

1. Improved Focus

The Matrix helps you increase personal and professional productivity. You can see where your priorities should sit and better concentrate on tasks with the greatest significance.

[15] Pres. Dwight Eisenhower in "Address at the Second Assembly of the World Council of Churches," Evanston, Illinois, August 19, 1954. Read the entire address at https://www.presidency.ucsb.edu/documents/address-the-second-assembly-the-world-council-churches-evanston-illinois, accessed August 14, 2024.

[16] Stephen R. Covey, *The Seven Habits of Highly Successful People*. New York City: Free Press (an imprint of Simon & Schuster), 1989.

2. Enhances Personal Management

It requires you to define goals and determine how individual activities further them. This distinction helps you avoid getting caught up in less important, albeit urgent, tasks.

3. Reduces Stress

Proactive planning and scheduling avoid last-minute rushes that lead to increased pressure, anxiety, and reduced quality. This approach enables you to manage your responsibilities more calmly and efficiently.

By controlling the effort you expend on your assigned tasks, you invest more time in those that genuinely contribute to your success and less on unproductive (although, at times, incredibly fun) activities. You achieve more, and your efforts will be more rewarding.

As previously noted, some actions are obvious: In a tornado emergency, for example, we (1) secure personnel safety, (2) secure the operational capability of the location and equipment, and (3) worry about the delivery schedule when we know how soon full operation can restart.

In normal operations, an owner or executive will have to sign the tax documents, but the bookkeeper or accountant will fill them out. HR might plan the company picnic, but the owner or manager will sign the checks. A secretary can screen applicants, but a manager or supervisor will make the hire.

You've probably noticed that these examples of doing or delegating are simple. Many others won't be, especially in smaller organizations. There could be judgement calls involved. You've probably also noticed that the Matrix is a paired absolute: Things are either urgent or not. Things are either important or they are not. That can be a problem for which I have a solution:

The Jochen Matrix—Eisenhower Enhanced

Real life is seldom black and white; there are shades of gray. (Yes, it's cliché, but we keep using them because they speak truths.) While Eisenhower divides only two ways. So, let's update the Eisenhower Matrix, using CARVER-like numbers to set priorities and gray-scale it for ease of comparison:

		URGENCY				
		TODAY (5)	THIS WEEK (4)	THIS MONTH (3)	THIS QUARTER (2)	BELOW MY PAY GRADE (1)
IMPORTANCE	I DO IT (4)	20	16	12	8	4
	I OVERSEE IT (3)	15	12	9	6	3
	I DELEGATE IT (2)	10	8	6	4	2
	BELOW MY PAY GRADE (1)	5	4	3	2	1

This new matrix increases the options for how management handles projects. It recognizes that urgency varies among projects. I should point out that, ultimately, nothing is below a top-tier leader's pay grade. That's simply a metaphor to assist leaders in avoiding the micro-management trap. Legal and other responsibilities don't end at middle management.

While the importance scale is reasonably universal, each management level may have an entirely different urgency scale: Shop supervisors may deal in hours, days, and weeks, while top-tier executives might deal in months, years, or even decades. The setting of response times can be crucial—whether in a business or other environment. Some examples of both:

Instinctive Responses — Short-Term

I wrote about instinctive or muscle memory responses in Chapter 3: Analyze the Threat. To summarize:

This response is generally appropriate to situations with a clear and present danger of considerable damage or injury if not dealt with immediately. Incidents that require immediate responses are, happily, exceedingly rare. In those high-pressure situations, instinct and muscle memory play huge roles. Training and repetitive practice help individuals automate their responses to potential scenarios. Responses may be needed within:

Seconds

- You're driving on the interstate and suddenly see someone driving the wrong way, coming towards you in your lane.
- You're attending a concert and hear gunshots.
- You start to sweat and feel chest pain.
- You discover an employee has embezzled funds.

Minutes

- On your way to the airport, you encounter a traffic jam and need an alternative route to catch your plane.
- You're confronted by your boss, who informs you that a major client has complained about your behavior.
- You have the feeling that the people in the car behind you are following you.

Hours

- You're on vacation, and it's raining all day, ruining your plans for a hike.
- A hurricane is approaching, and the authorities announce a mandatory evacuation is possible.
- A customer calls and complains about the inferior quality of the products you recently delivered, which are causing problems in his assembly lines.
- A strike against your trucking company shuts them down, and they can't complete critical deliveries.

Tactical Responses — Mid-Term

Life and death scenarios aside, life generally gives you time to plan a response or to implement a response already planned, tailoring it to the specifics of the situation. You can't fix these situations in a day or a week. They may require extensive intelligence gathering before a successful resolution can be determined and implemented:

Days

- Your working hours are reduced, and you must adjust your budget for food, cars, and other expenses.
- A significant customer is late with a substantial payment.
- Market research shows that the demand for a new product in development has decreased over the past few months.

Weeks

- You notice your child's behavior is changing; he or she gets angry all the time for no apparent reason.
- The boss spends less time in his office and more time wandering around the shop and other areas, looking at everything but saying nothing.
- Crime in your neighborhood increases, and there are more home invasions than ever before.

Months

Some decisions will need implementation, testing, evaluation, and revision before reaching a final solution. Use that time to obtain internal and external opinions, where appropriate:

- Developing a business plan for a new startup or product line.
- Catching up to a company that's just brought a new and improved device to market that directly competes with one of yours.
- The employee turnover in your company is decreasing.
- A new tax code is enacted, which will take effect at the beginning of the following calendar year.

- Inflation raises prices; each paycheck seems to buy less, and your income will no longer support your current lifestyle.

In all cases, you don't have to create a written plan before engaging in mitigation efforts. You can, and probably should, make notes on whatever you're dealing with. The situation might arise again, and you'll want to be more ready than you were this time. In most families and organizations, some problems are easily foreseeable, and some legal or business requirements are mandatory in any crisis. Every business or organization should create a standard crisis response checklist.

The crisis management plan will often evolve as the situation develops. Some corrections will happen faster than expected, and some will be slower. Many efforts will affect others. As the situation progresses, regardless of whether that happens in days or weeks, the crisis response team will draft a comprehensive assessment document utilizing MDMP, the OODA Loop, the Ishikawa Diagrams, the Jochen Matrix, and any other tools they find useful. That plan would record mitigation and recovery efforts and recommend changes in procedure, technology, and even corporate culture if that culture contributed to the problem. (See Scenario 26 on p. 123.)

The comprehensive assessment document will, of course, be an evolving document. For example, your initial engineering report might suggest a minor flaw, but follow-up examinations could show deeper issues. Legal will probably revise its strategy if a few individual lawsuits are filed and consolidated into a class-action suit. If internal documents are discovered that reveal pre-production knowledge of the flaw, human resources will definitely expand their outboarding plans.

Flexibility

> The best-laid schemes o' mice an' men Gang aft agley.
> (The best laid plans of mice and men ofttimes go awry.)
>
> —Robert Burns[17]

[17] Robert Burns, "To a Mouse, On Turning Her Up in Her Nest with the Plough," *Poems, Chiefly in the Scottish Dialect* (commonly known as the *Kilmarnock Edition*), November 1785.

The world is unpredictable; even the most carefully crafted plans can face hitches. Flexibility is as crucial as the plan itself. Being adaptable doesn't mean you're deviating from your objective; it means you're nimble in your approach to reaching your objective.

1. Regularly Review

Once your plan is in motion, regularly reassess the situation. Is everything going according to plan? Certainly not, so what adjustments are needed?

2. Stay Open to Input

If you're in a group, be receptive to feedback or suggestions. Collective wisdom can often see what one person might overlook.

3. Recognize There Are Unknowns

Understand that you won't have all the answers, and surprises might emerge. Being mentally prepared for these will allow you to pivot your plan without succumbing to panic again. Remember:

- Planning is your roadmap out of panic.
- Strategy converts reactive impulses into proactive actions.
- Remember that a good plan today is better than a perfect plan tomorrow.
- Be swift, be strategic, but most importantly, be adaptable.

Monitoring the Situation

Those revisions will be of most value when the management and recovery efforts are fully and adequately monitored. Businesses speak frequently of "key performance indicators" (KPIs). At each stage of recovery, KPIs should be set to describe what success looks like. Costs, for example, are significant KPIs. In all businesses, the bottom line counts. In the mid-term recovery phase, you may look like you're fixing the problem in the most efficient and effective method, however, every dollar a recovery plan spends is a dollar deducted from your profits. "How long will it take for us to earn enough profit to pay the costs of recovery?" is a question that should be on everyone's mind, not just the bookkeepers.

When the quarterly or annual reports are published, if you have to say, "Well, this problem cost us $100,000 in lost business, and we spent $300,000 to fix it," you'll have to earn an extra $400,000 to cover those losses. (Tax considerations aside, this is not good news.)

If, instead, the report read, "Well, this crisis cost us $100,000 in lost business, so we immediately put a solution in place. As the situation developed, it became clear that this solution would cost us $300,000, so we stopped, reviewed our intelligence, and modified our plan. Ultimately, the recovery cost only $125,000." That is still a significant loss, but one the stockholders will find much easier to live with.

Strategic Responses — Long-term Recovery & Prevention Plans

The key to long-term recovery is prevention planning. Repeating that old sage, "***It costs you nothing to correct a mistake that never gets made.***" I cover this in detail in Chapter 6: Improve with an Eye to the Future. For now:

Real World Examples

Scenario 26: The Ford Pinto

The late 1960s saw the introduction of the Ford Pinto, a direct competitor to the emerging Japanese small car options. The design and prototype phases went well, but during product testing, low-speed rear-end collisions produced gas tank explosions. Undeniably, it is a serious situation. Ford considered a couple of options: Reposition the tank above the axle, as in the Ford Capri, or reinforce the tank to prevent the leaks causing the fires. In a fantastic episode of corporate denial, Ford did nothing because the cost of reengineering and the rollout delay would've been more than twice the cost of the anticipated costs of injury and death claims. The car went onto showroom floors in 1971.

As noted previously, secrets eventually get out. The US National Highway Traffic Safety Administration began investigating fuel tank complaints and general dangers of the car. Soon after, journalists uncovered internal Ford documents detailing their knowledge of the danger. Lawsuits ensued, damages were paid, and the vehicles were recalled and repaired, but the damage to Ford's public image lasted far longer than any other factor. The Pinto line was dropped in 1980.

By the way, some subsequent investigations have suggested that the Pinto problem, though serious (death estimates ranging up to about 200 were common), wasn't as serious as the media and the lawsuits alleged (claims of 500 to 900 deaths were made but never proven). I mention this to point out, historically, that the media has its agenda, and they are not your ally.

Scenario 27: The Alloy

There was a flood in central Europe—a small creek became a raging river within minutes—and that river flooded an industrial zone. Unfortunately, this industrial zone produced a specific alloy used by a supplier to make car body sections for several car manufacturers.

This factory was the only source of that alloy, a fact manufacturers paid no attention to because it was a second-tier supplier. Many large manufacturers don't deal with their second tiers. They deal with their first tiers and depend on the first tiers to keep an eye on the second tiers.

So, we have complete dependency on this single supplier, and those supplies suddenly became unavailable for an estimated two weeks or more while the locals cleaned up after the flood. My company was called in to do the recovery planning and assist with business continuity because the manufacturers couldn't stop building cars. We needed a solution, and we needed it quickly. With the primary supplier completely unavailable, we had to find another supplier who could produce that alloy in the quantities we required and move all the raw materials to their location.

That took some creative thinking and research to locate a very out-of-the-box solution: We found a new supplier that was, inconveniently, based in another country. We hired a dedicated train—a huge, long train—to transport the raw materials to the alternate supplier, some 1600 kilometers—almost a thousand miles away.

We didn't do it on our own; of course, sub-contractors did the actual labor. We used a service company that usually moves heavy industry production machines. Those people transported all the raw materials to the station and loaded the train. Then, the train, hired from a national rail line, rolled to the new location. The train was unloaded at the factory by another subcontractor. Finally, that new factory continued production.

All this had to be set up as quickly as humanly possible to minimize the economic damage that would result from those manufacturers not producing a single car for two and a half weeks.

Scenario 28: The Katrina Evacuation

You may remember Hurricane Katrina and the devastation it caused to New Orleans and every person for over 100 miles in every direction. Many had to be evacuated out of the State of Louisiana because there was no way to provide services for all of them in-state. Many of the people who fled ended up with a genuine problem: No paperwork.

Because of the speed of the spreading flood, they had no time to create an emergency plan; they just ran for their lives. They left behind bank info, birth certificates, home ownership documents, insurance papers, professional and trade licenses, and much more. Many of them only had their driver's licenses, car registrations, and credit or debit cards because those were in their wallet, pocket, or cars. Many did not think to grab family history documents, photos, the household bills they had to pay, and so forth. Even computers were left behind.

Many of those documents were lost in the flood. For those who'd been evacuated from Louisiana to other states, it took time to get replacements because the system wasn't designed to deal with hundreds of thousands of replacement requests in so short a time. The displaced overwhelmed the system.

Insurance payments, government benefits, obtaining new employment for those who decided not to return home, and more were delayed. In all cases, these are replaceable documents, in considerable measure because we have internet access to financial and professional service providers but, it still takes time and, in crisis situations of Katrina's magnitude—most of the USA was affected directly or indirectly, everything seems to slow down because of the sheer volume of people who need help.

If you haven't heard of a "bug-out bag," there are numerous websites that can offer advice as to their content. Besides essentials like water, food, flashlight, first aid kit, handgun, and ammunition, we recommend a USB drive with images of all necessary documents, family photos, work records, and so on. Also, where do you go if you have to evacuate your home? Deciding where beforehand (to friends or relatives, for example) will reduce a great deal of stress and fear in disaster situations. For businesses, it's tougher because shops need machinery, and professional services need computers and internet bandwidth, but those are not impossible to arrange.

On any basis—personal, business, or community—preparation is the key to survival.

Communication

Public communication, that is, all information disseminated by the company or organization to the general population—must operate under three principles:

Need-to-Know

One of journalism's favorite justifications for sticking their noses where said noses don't belong is, "The public has a right to know." I concede the point with two vital caveats:

1. I am not in any way obligated to assist the "Fourth Estate," as journalists like to call themselves, in collecting or publishing any information. In most companies, I'm obligated ***not to assist*** because of non-disclosure agreements (NDAs) or other contractual obligations.
2. The right to know does not imply a need-to-know. Companies and organizations have as much right to privacy as any person, and they have confidential information that, if published, could damage or destroy them. The law protects trade secrets and other confidential data as definitely as it protects personal information.

Clarity

> We should not write so that it is possible for the reader to understand us, but so that it is impossible for him to misunderstand us.
>
> —Quintilian[18]

Anyone who's heard political interviews has heard journalists ask, as a follow-up question, "Do you mean…" and then suggest something the politician most definitely did not mean. They also do it to business spokespersons and others. This is entrapment, designed to elicit an answer they want, regardless of the truth.

When making information about your organization public, it must be crafted carefully designed with such adherence to strict parameters that the engineering staff would be envious of their exactness. The facts must be presented at the right time, via the right platform, to the right people. So, hire top-level writers and pay them what they're worth to avoid escalating a problem into a crisis. It's a small investment compared to damage control.

The Press Conference

Preparation

When a public press conference (a "presser," in the jargon of the trade) is necessary, prepare!

- You should invite every significant media outlet to the location of the incident. Doing otherwise suggests favoritism. You should collect the names and contact info of the right people in each outlet—city desk, business desk, healthcare desk, whoever should be invited.
- What questions are they likely to ask? What are the minimal facts you can share to answer the question honestly without violating company privacy? What should you not say?

[18] Often attributed to Mark Twain or other modern thinkers, it was first penned by Marcus Fabius Quintilianus, *Institutes of Eloquence*, Book 8, Chapter 2, c. AD 95. (Born c. AD 35 and died c. AD100, Quintillian was a Roman educator & rhetorician, the teacher of Pliny the Younger and, perhaps, of Tacitus.)

- Don't hurry; they will come to hear you. Print, radio, and television outlets still have deadlines, but the internet has given us the capability to receive 24/7 updates, so act on your timetable, not theirs. When they ask a question, don't hesitate to ask them to repeat, rephrase, pause, and think for a second before answering.
- Keep control over the conversation, answer briefly and clearly, and answer exactly the questions they ask, but volunteer nothing. If they quote you, it'll be a soundbite—prep several in advance.

Execution

New to being a "spox" or spokesperson? Watch a few pressers, imitate what works well, and don't repeat others' mistakes. The Israelis, who always face a hostile world press, have become particular masters of the iconic "presser" non-communication style. They're exceptionally skilled instructors in the art. Some quintessential responses are:

- "I don't know." If you don't have facts, say so without hesitation. They'll ask why. "Those decisions are not yet final," or something like that is a perfectly legitimate response. Refuse to offer opinions or speculate. When you're done, say, "Ladies and gentlemen, thank you for your time. There will be further updates when additional information is available." Then, walk away and don't turn back. (Whenever possible, set the room up so you have a separate exit.)
- "We neither confirm nor deny." This phrase, a standard among government agencies worldwide, is honest and open without compromising data that should not be shared.
- "We do not discuss operational details." A straightforward, tactical way to shut down questions without providing any insight.
- "Israel will do what Israel has to do." This statement asserts Israel's right to act independently in protecting its security interests without specifying those actions.
- "We don't talk about this, and we don't talk about why we don't talk about it." That declaration (my personal favourite) epitomizes the approach of pushing certain matters entirely

off the table. It discourages follow-up questions as it conveys that the topic is beyond public discussion.

Israel's well-practiced, cryptic communication style can be easily adapted to risk and crisis management in commercial circumstances under a general principle:

- "We're managing the situation; the details aren't open for discussion."

This line asserts control over a crisis and signals that steps are being taken but says nothing of the specifics. It reassures stakeholders that the company handles the issue without giving sensitive operational insights. Likewise:

- "Our approach here is best left unsaid, and we've been clear on why we're not saying it." This communicates that sensitive issues are not open to discussion, protecting corporate strategy while making it clear that nondisclosure is intentional.
- "We'll do what's necessary to protect our interests." This phrase declares that actions are being taken to mitigate or eliminate corporate risks, signaling a proactive approach but leaving out operational details.
- "In this matter, discretion is part of our strategy," or "As a policy, we do not discuss our internal risk management measures." Designed for high-stakes risk management situations, these lines affirm that confidentiality is an intentional part of the company approach by directly but politely affirming the company's right to privacy.

Everybody Has an Agenda

Your company has an agenda—in corporate terms, your goals and objectives. Governments, charities, and individuals have agendas.

Media outlets also have agendas. In a crisis situation, always assume that ***their*** agenda is not ***your*** agenda—better yet, that ***their*** agenda is in conflict with ***your*** agenda. (Again, act under the protection of a measured paranoia.) This leads to a brief history lesson:

> Congress shall make no law respecting an establishment of religion or prohibiting the free exercise thereof; ***or abridging the freedom of speech, or of the press***; or the right of the people peaceably to assemble, and to petition the Government for a redress of grievances.
>
> —The Constitution of the United States, 1st Article of Amendment (emphasis added)[19]

Freedom of the press in the United States was given constitutional protection because the Founders knew journalistic objectivity was a myth. In the 18th Century, any person or group with a little money could buy paper and a press and publish what they wanted.

Today, the internet has made that dream almost cost-free, resulting in a tsunami of bloggers and would-be influencers spouting both wisdom and nonsense. This level of freedom would warm the hearts of the Founders as surely as it would turn their stomachs. They felt their new republic couldn't survive if the information were controlled by the government, so they decided they could live with the mayhem of a free press because they were sure their new republic could not live without it.

That was a long route to a short answer to a vital question: Is the media your friend or ally?

The answer is a resounding, "Oh, ***hell***, no!"

The media's public agenda—"finding and publishing the truth" is as much a myth as it was three centuries ago.

Media outlets are businesses, and their agenda is profit. Keep in mind the old adage, "If it bleeds, it leads." Bad news sells better than good news most of the time. (That says something about our culture, and it's not complimentary.) Each of them competes intensely with every other outlet to sell papers, magazines, or ads. They're after the "scoop"—something they know that the rest of their industry doesn't—and some have no morality in how they get it. Some even invent it.

Media outlets are also influencers—social engineering firms—and their agenda is power. They propagandize for whoever holds their purse strings. They promote the social causes and political platforms

[19] Submitted to the several States on September 25, 1789. Ratification completed on December 15, 1791.

their owners want promoted. They highlight anything that forwards those causes or platforms and ignore the rest of the day's news. Or they lie about it.

This raging outburst isn't here because I don't like or trust modern media. (I don't, but that's beside the point.) This book is about dealing with crises. Earlier, I mentioned that law enforcement suspects everyone is guilty when they arrive at a crime scene. They gather evidence that pulls people off the suspect list or raises them toward the top. When you're in crisis, do likewise: Assume that everyone could be a hindrance to successfully surviving that crisis until you've proven to yourself that they'll be of help. (And remember, just because they helped last time doesn't guarantee they'll help this time.)

General Advice

There are times when you should encourage the community to help solve the problem. When a hiker goes missing, the whole town may turn out to help search. When technology problems arise, professional associations may know people who can help you; suppliers and suppliers of suppliers may have useful insights; former employees might've run into this problem or something similar; talk to the lawyers—always the lawyers!

As a general rule, I suggest: Share your problems with as many as necessary, as few as possible.

Resource Management

Crises have costs—money, time, materials, people. You can't escape those costs, but effective allocation and utilization of resources can lower them.

Remember, there are mistakes that lead to problems which can evolve into crises. Among other tools, careful oversight of all resources can identify a coming crisis while still in the problem stage or before. There are numerous resources that, based on the situation, might need careful management.

Corporate Culture

It has been suggested that a company's most valuable resource is its personnel. I concur.

Years ago, a specialty chocolate company had a small fire at the beginning of their Christmas rush. This, by itself, didn't create a crisis but local laws were extremely strict where food was concerned. The fire was caused by a short in one of the production machines, which produced a quantity of smoke. That smoke contaminated all the products in the production room and all the plastic molds from which they were made.

The entire production batch—several hundred pounds of premium chocolate—had to be destroyed, along with the molds. Fortunately, the patterns from which the molds were made, as well as all the products completed before the fire, were stored elsewhere and were unaffected. However, new molds had to be made, and the contaminated product replaced. The company's lifeblood was the Christmas employee-gift season, so there was no room for error; the product had to ship on time.

The production manager got everybody together, both the shop and shipping people. He laid out the details of the situation, explained what happened, and what they'd have to do to catch up. With the assistance of all available shipping people, shop people would have to work until the job was done. If delivery dates were missed, the company might permanently lose customers. Those clients had paid their money; they were expecting their product as promised because, for those clients, these gifts were a matter of their employees' morale. (In some cases, it was a company tradition stretching back years.)

Everybody (mostly temporary workers who came on for three or four months a year) raised their hand and said, "We're in. We'll work seven days a week if we have to." Many worked 12-hour days, six days a week for two weeks. Their efficiency was such that they got everything caught up far faster than anyone expected. The workers took a potential disaster and made a miracle.

Many of these seasonal workers were repeaters—they returned every fall to meet the Christmas rush, doing other things in winter, spring, and summer. If the owner and managers hadn't treated those workers well, they wouldn't return with a commitment to keep the company's excellent reputation intact. A full crew of inexperienced seasonals wouldn't have been up to the challenge.

A positive corporate culture saved the company.

Prioritize

What needs and resources must be expended? In an individual or community crisis, ask yourself vital questions and listen to the answers:

- What can kill you in three minutes? You need a first aid kit.
- What can kill you in an hour to a day? You need basic self-defense tools, clothing, and environmental protection.
- What can kill you in three days? You need clean water or a way to clean the water around you.
- What can kill you in three weeks? You need food, preferably in easy-to-move, no-refrigeration-needed packaging.
- For all of the above, you need training in how to use these resources most effectively, and whenever possible, you should have a friend or two to watch your back.

Needless to say—which is why I'm saying it clearly here—none of this just happens. When the crisis hits, it's too late to put a bug-out bag together or take a first aid class.

The Pareto Principle

Resources must be allocated according to risks and benefits. In 1906, Italian intellectual Vilfredo Pareto wrote that 80 percent of Italy's wealth was in the hands of just 20 percent of the population. In 1941, Romanian-American engineer Joseph Juran applied Pareto's observation to businesses and concluded that 80 percent of any issue is caused by 20 percent of quality issues. Later, it was also noted that "20 percent of the budget kills 80 percent of the problem." (Assuming, of course, that the budget is allocated properly.)

Eventually, Juran coined the term "the Pareto Principle," calling the split "the vital few and the useful many," highlighting the value of the greater contribution without disparaging the necessity of the lesser contributions.

"The 80/20 Rule," as it's most commonly called today (also "The Law of the Vital Few" or "The Principle of Factor Sparsity"), has become doctrine in most sectors. Where multiple causes are identified in a crisis—and this is not rare—the Pareto Principle can be a useful tool in determining where resources are to be apportioned.

Rational Self-Interest

"Look out for number one," as many have advised, is usually a good thing. You can't, after all, help others if you are not secure. But it can easily be taken too far—don't overproduce or overbuy.

In the early days of the COVID lockdowns, for example, Americans bought toilet paper like it was whiskey, and prohibition had just been re-introduced. (Hoard toilet paper because of a respiratory ailment? Not a decision I would've advised.) At the same time, several distillers switched temporarily from alcoholic beverages to hand sanitizer to meet the expected demand.

"Expected" became the operative word. Months went by, and the panic buying quieted. Many people tried to return cases of toilet paper to their local grocery stores, only to find those stores had all the products they needed. At the same time, so much hand sanitizer had been produced that shopping carts were filled with unwanted bottles being given away for free.

COVID was an exceptional case. All the alleged experts told the same story, so most of us believed them instead of performing our own due diligence and researching the truth for ourselves. Some who acted on the "expert" advice found themselves regretting it.

Like elsewhere, intelligence is a vital resource to be managed, but information can be wrong. In cases where there is controversy, you must, ultimately, trust your research and gut.

A Few Miscellaneous Rules

Once the crisis is defined, determine if you can solve it internally or if you need external specialists. (It's never a bad idea to make that phone call and see what the experts offer.)

Check resources currently available against those you know you'll need. Define and close that gap.

Establish a budget for all resources and do it in planning. You may not be able to effectively budget later.

Allocate resources properly and in a timely manner and get the right tools for your situation.

Allocate according to needs and reallocate according to the changing circumstances, as needed. Re-budget according to the changing circumstances, as required. Always collaborate and coordinate with other stakeholders.

Decide early who needs to know and keep them updated on a regular basis. They can't help if they don't know the situation.

Monitor and control everything, especially money.

Evaluate constantly; adapt as needed.

Chapter 6

Improve with an Eye to the Future

Earlier, I mentioned several key points, including:

- When fighting a fire, one must extinguish all the embers, or the fire may flare up again.
- Too many people deal with the obvious, the symptoms of a problem, and fail to dig deeper to get to the root cause of the problem.
- Situational awareness, the 5-Why method, and other tools help you past proximal causes to reach ultimate causes.

Risk and crisis management deal with taking on demanding situations and mitigating or eliminating threats to personal, corporate, or community safety. From all these situations, we can learn. If we fail to learn enough, that is, if we don't consider ways to help prevent a recurrence of whatever threat we've just overcome, the job is only half-done.

A Word of Warning

Some problems have no solution. Certain situations have existed in the world for so long, and the roots of those situations go so deep that the human condition or psyche will have to undergo fundamental changes before we have any chance of eliminating these problems. For example:

1. Crime—Organized and Individual

The Cartels, the Mafia, the Tongs, the Yakuza, the small-time gangs that never earn so much attention that we remember their names: there will always be those who break the law because they think they can get away with it. Crime continues because they're often right in the short term. The more successful among those who misbehave are those who understand the power of group action. Sadly, destroy any mob or gang and something will spring up within days, even hours, to replace it.

Crime, however, is a business; profit and loss, market share, competition, and so on are the same challenges facing commercial (i.e., legal) operations. Where crime cannot make a profit, they leave or go broke. Strong cooperation among resident and business populations, law enforcement and other agencies, and the political establishment can make a neighborhood, a city, or even a state less profitable. It's never a complete or permanent solution, but it helps.

2. Ethnic-Nationalistic-Religious Conflict

The struggles between Arabs and Israelis, between Armenians and Turks, between China and Japan, between India and Pakistan, between every ***us*** and ***them*** community that comprises humanity have existed far longer than civilized societies have kept records. One might wonder if any of these groups actually exterminated their supposed "opponents," would they settle down or just go looking for another group to victimize?

3. Prejudice in General

Over 150 years ago, an amendment to the United States Constitution outlawed slavery. Everybody involved, as perpetrator or victim, is long dead. Still, the subject rises like the sun (meaning every day) somewhere in American political rhetoric and social experience.

It's not a uniquely American problem, though many might try to convince you it is. Almost all the conflict in society is rooted in a simple misconception: You are different; therefore, you are inferior; thus, you must be converted or exterminated or "kept down"—or some other damn-fool idea.

The rioting we've all seen all over Europe and North America in 2023 and 2024 (as this book is being written) has different players on the stage. Still, the text is the same as the one we saw in America in the 1960s. It bears little, if any, difference to the ethnic troubles we saw as far back as the 7th Century BCE when the Babylonians expelled the Jews from their land.

These globe-girdling problems seem far removed from everyday business until the rioting comes to your street or voices call for your products to be boycotted because of some connection to someone or something they don't like.

4. Illnesses, Injuries, & Miscellaneous Calamities

Moses once said, "Would God that all the Lord's people were prophets." Well, divine desire aside, we are not all prophets; the future comes as it comes and, sometimes, in unexpectedly horrifying ways. Illnesses, injuries, and other troubles can arise without warning and, often, without any logic or explanation.

Losing any individual in a company of 100,000-plus does not, generally, initiate a crisis. What about a key employee in a company of 25 or 30? What about a group that spends months or years preparing to open a business, only to see the lead entrepreneur diagnosed with stage-4 cancer and pass away before the business is firmly organized? What about a family who loses a father or mother in a car accident?

As the title suggests, hardships occur, and we must rise above them with resilience to achieve a breakthrough. In business, it's often easy to walk away from a deal that no longer has a path to success, requires compromising principles, or involves criminality. In life, walking away is not always an option.

The proverb says, "That which cannot be cured must be endured." Agreed. However, could we honestly call ourselves civilized beings or adults if we did not continue to try?

Strategic Responses — Long-term — Recovery & Prevention Plans

Chapter 5 dealt with instinctive and tactical responses—fixing the crisis. Once the immediate situation is under control, recovery must walk hand-in-hand with prevention. (Technically, the mid-term and long-term responses will overlap, but I'm confident you can handle it!)

Preparation

Preparation, as I have written, can mitigate many disastrous situations. I also mentioned a "bug-out bag" containing things you'll need to take in case some disaster requires you to evacuate your home on short notice. Businesses should have similar plans:

- Funds can be held in precious metals or other negotiable instruments in a bank or other secure off-site location.
- Computer files can be backed up to "the cloud" or another off-site server in case of a cyber-attack or hardware damage.
- Make a spare. If you have molds or patterns, create a spare set, if possible, and keep that set with your emergency funds and off-site server.
- Large-scale physical property is harder to protect than intellectual property or small, mobile equipment. The right insurance policy can't help you protect it, but it can help you replace it. Insurance reviews should happen annually or whenever you make significant changes.

Every business should put some time into risk management, that is, planning. You can't imagine every problem that might arise, but you aren't the first to face disaster; it's happened many times to others. The internet is full of articles and videos, and libraries-bookstores are full of books on how people dealt with crises. Learn from other people's mistakes and successes. You could even call on experts like my firm to assist in a risk-management survey.

Now, you may say, "Well, I'm a really small business. Risk management would take time away from making money. In fact, it would cost me money, and I can't afford it." Really? You pay for insurance on your life, home, car, and (I hope) business, even though your fondest dream is to pass away, never having used any of them. Is risk management, as an idea, any different from insurance? Actually, in one way, they are remarkably similar and, in another, almost exact opposites: Insurance can only help you recover after a crisis hits, as crisis management can help. However, a crisis management plan can also assist you in preventing a recurrence of disaster and, even more exciting, can assist you in preventing the first occurrence.

Intelligence

Prevention is the long-term goal of recovery. Real prevention is based on discerning the root causes of problems and ensuring those situations are solved until they are so gone that they dare not regain their ugly heads in your presence. To be effective, as with all other aspects of risk and crisis management, recovery and prevention key to intelligence.

After stabilizing the situation, the company should make a detailed assessment, identifying the root causes, any markers that indicated a crash was coming, the full details of the situation, information on the impact and effects, and how you dealt with them. Performing a root cause analysis should include the structural damage, potential financial losses, impacts on stakeholders, and the company culture.

For example, in a data breach, implement whatever changes are required to seal the breach while determining the cause and identifying the vulnerabilities that lead to it. Assess the impact, financial losses, loss of reputation, and other damages.

Now, with the root cause and probable effects identified, develop a course of action and action plan to address each problem and restore normal business operations. That restoration may include dealing with a huge backlog of client projects. Overtime is expensive, but how much more expensive would it be to lose long-time clients and be forced to hunt for new ones?

The After-Action Review (AAR)

One member of the crisis management team should be designated on day one to receive and compile all these reports and create the AAR. In creating that report, remember two things:

1. The First Rule of Journalism—Trust but verify. Collect every document, take many, many photographs, video every interview, gather news reports and outside commentary, make a copy of everything, and place it in a secure, off-site location.
2. The Five Questions of Journalism—What happened? Who made it happen? When did it happen? Where did it happen? Why is it significant? (That last question is often phrased: Why should I care?)

This collection isn't the AAR; it's the raw data the crisis team will use to compile the AAR. It is a brief but informative document that explains the crisis and recommends preventative measures.

Once normal operations are restored, one must look to the future. Root causes, vulnerabilities, security glitches, or whatever other problems led to the breach must be addressed in-house or by consulting crisis experts. They'll outline the steps needed to eliminate those roots and increase the resilience of your system. Whether new clients or existing ones, a thorough prevention plan will improve client confidence.

Corporate Culture

As I previously mentioned, personnel is a vital resource for crisis response management. Your people can also be key players in prevention. Suppose that, in a manufacturing shop, plans for a new assembly hit the shop floor. Everybody turns to and works enthusiastically to get the new products off to the customers. After a couple of days, a shop worker looks at what she's doing and frowns. "This bolt," she thinks, "doesn't look big enough to hold these two parts together under the strain to be put on this assembly." She goes to the shop foreman and explains her concerns.

"The engineers tested it thoroughly," the foreman says, "They're sure it'll hold forever."

"I understand," she replies, "but I've been doing this for two decades. My gut says this bolt isn't big enough to hold the strain on this joint."

In a positive corporate culture, the foreman trusts her experience and talks to the production manager. That manager knows it'll cost time and money to test the assembly, but he trusts his people. He calls the general manager, who authorizes a shop shutdown and additional testing.

Sure enough, the engineers missed their mark. They tested the assembly in a controlled environment instead of an actual-use scenario, and the bolt breaks. The assembler, foreman, and production manager were rewarded ***publicly*** for trusting their experience; the engineers were ***quietly*** reprimanded for incomplete testing protocols. The assembly was quickly redesigned to accommodate a larger bolt, and the customer never knew what didn't hit them.

In many other companies, the opposite could've happened. Some supervisors and managers don't want to hear about problems, some executives care more about degrees than first-hand experience, and some engineers don't care what a shop jockey's gut says. Also, let's be honest: a crisis was not inevitable in this scenario—the shop jockey's gut might've been wrong.

Change Direction

As one plans for or deals with a crisis, one may conclude that what their organization is doing isn't working or isn't working as well as it could. New directions shouldn't be feared; they should be embraced as opportunities for growth. (In making such a consideration, it's well to recall a joke by an old sage, "Politicians often speak of taking the state or the nation in a new [and unspecified] direction. 'Straight to hell' is, usually, a new direction, but not one to be desired.) Here are a couple of simple examples:

Scenario 29: Tape

In 1912, Thomas Edison was annoyed. The cardboard box had recently become available and, like previous packages, was closed with twine. Edison was bothered by the time it took to twine up a box and the fact that the boxes never really closed fully. He, therefore, devised a water-activated packaging tape. It was a huge breakthrough. It allowed people to thoroughly seal a carton rather than hold it closed. The idea wasn't perfect, but someone else built on Edison's idea by creating a dispenser with a reservoir and sponge—an efficient way to dampen and cut the tape. Later, fiberglass strands were incorporated to strengthen the tape. Over 110 years later, millions of factories, shippers, and warehouses still use that same basic product.

Scenario 30: Rice

In the early years of Israel's modern existence, austerity was necessary. Rice, among other things, was in short supply. Then-Prime Minister David Ben-Gurion called for a solution. Food engineers at a company called Osem produced something new: Called *ptitim*—from an Arabic word for "pounding dry bread"—this roasted wheat flour paste soon caught on with Israeli consumers. The austerity period ended, but *ptitim* remains a staple of Israeli children's diet.

In a strange twist, in recent years, this stop-gap staple food replacement has gained favor as a gourmet ingredient in cuisines worldwide.

Scenario 31: Porridge

When droughts and other food crises hit under-developed nations, food producers around the world donate generously. Unfortunately, those suffering from malnutrition, children and seniors in particular, often have compromised systems that can't digest whole grains or foods made with coarse flour. *Atmit* (an Arab word for "thin, nourishing porridge") had been around for centuries and was an excellent option for those who needed it. Unfortunately, primitive production methods kept it from fulfilling its full potential as an emergency food. Even so, in 2003, The Church of Jesus Christ of Latter-day Saints Welfare Services (LDSWS) began producing *atmit* for donation to crisis areas.

In 2009, LDSWS asked food scientists at the Church-owned Brigham Young University to create a modern formula for the porridge. Two years of research produced a shelf-stable blend with additional nutrients not found in traditional recipes. Since then, thousands of tons have been donated to countries at risk in North and South America, Africa, and Asia, with marvelous results.

Reassessment & Reallocation

Negative effects of a crisis can be numerous. In the shopping mall shooter example, the incident was short, but the effects could be long for some. None of the victims left home that morning expecting to be shot at. The young hero didn't leave home expecting to take a life.

Post-Traumatic Stress Disorder (PTSD) is real, it hurts, and it's not just the successor to the so-called "battle fatigue" experienced by World War II soldiers or the "shell shock" that hit them after World War I. It's no surprise that assault, child abuse, rape, and other crimes can leave indelible impressions on one's psyche. Accidents, divorces, severe illnesses, or injuries—any situation that grabs you by the throat and throws you out of your comfort zone, can push you over the psychological edge. It's become routine for schools, law enforcement agencies, and the military to offer psychological counseling in the aftermath of traumatic events. Many businesses also offer mental health services as part of their compensation packages.

Economic and financial changes have always been part of the "new normal" that results from crises. I've already mentioned the costs of lost business, repairs, recertifications, and other things. This might mean reduced wages and salaries for a time, no profits to share, 401K matching funds unavailable, and so on.

Depending on the size of the organization, owners and managers need to lead on this and should not sacrifice in equal measure to hourly staff. An executive making $180,000 per year should not be expected to take the same pay cut as a shop floor worker making $60,000. Granted, the executive may be "more valuable" with skill sets and experience that far outshines the shop jockey, but in a crisis that threatens the future of the company, we're not talking about value; we're talking about survival. If the company doesn't make it through, you'll both be getting a 100 percent reduction in pay.

If it's a choice between pay reductions and layoffs, the shop jockeys need to be heard on that decision. Some who have their years in might be inclined to take an early retirement deal—a frequent choice during the COVID lockdowns. Others may have some flexibility—a two-income household faces a different situation than a one-income household. Others still may see an opportunity to go in another direction and leave voluntarily. You don't know unless you ask, so ask!

A Rebuilding Year

Professional sports teams losing key players to retirement or other reasons often face the expectation of a less-than-successful season as fresh players or new coaches get integrated with the old. Businesses surviving a crisis may have a comparable situation. As part of long-term planning, the business should look at options that can enhance their prevention plan:

- Training. New information and skills cost money, but if it lessens the chance of a recurring crisis, it's money well spent.
- Infrastructure. If physical damage has been done, should you take the insurance money and restore, rebuild, or upgrade machines, buildings, or other stuff?
- Should the company institute new policies, processes, governance, or oversight SOPs?
- Was the crisis management effective? Should the company rethink its risk management program?
- What did we miss? Did our insurance cover everything? Can we outsource some of our risk to subcontractors?
- Crises reveal the true nature of relationships. Who helped? Who ignored? Who hurt?

I never recommend revenge, and we note that companies have taken revenge on stakeholders who don't support them "properly." Indeed, there should be rewards of some kind for those who worked hard to get the company through a crisis. But backlash can backfire because, down the road, you may need those stakeholders.

Preventing Disasters

How do you identify and address minor issues before they escalate into major crises? By leveraging key principles and KPIs for business excellence.

Heinrich's Law

In my experience working with major clients—crises rarely stem from a single catastrophic event. Instead, they unfold as a series of smaller issues that, when combined, create significant problems.

> The ratios graphically portrayed above—1:29:300—show that, in a unit group of 330 similar accidents, 300 will produce no injury whatever, 29 will result in only minor injuries, and one will result seriously.
>
> —Herbert William Heinrich[20]

Obviously, industrial safety practices have improved greatly in the last century, so Heinrich has been revisited and revised many times. Still, this first industrial safety warning is a worthwhile reminder that small problems, left unaddressed, can escalate into crises and that small issues, properly addressed, can reduce or eliminate many risks.

It's also crucial for leaders to proactively address minor issues. It's been said that "Perfect is the enemy of good." Attributed to the French philosopher Voltaire, who advised that striving for a flawless situation can stifle creativity and entrepreneurship. Voltaire sought balance—eliminating critical issues without becoming obsessed over what's now known as "the small stuff."

The Domino Theory

Part of Heinrich's work concluded that accidents occurred because events or conditions happen in a specific sequence:[21]

[20] Herbert Heinrich, *Industrial Accident Prevention: A Scientific Approach*. New York City: McGraw-Hill Book Co. Inc., 1931.
[21] *Ibid.*

1. Ancestry and Social Environment

Humans are naturally cautious, but some people are raised in environments that promote reckless behaviors.

2. Fault of Person

Persons raised in reckless environments become reckless people.

3. Unsafe Acts/Mechanical and Physical Hazards

Reckless behavior, combined with unguarded gears or the absence of safety rails, results directly in accidents.

4. Accidents

People falling, being struck by flying objects, etc., cause injuries.

5. Injury

Fractures, lacerations, etc., result from accidents.

The Domino Effect

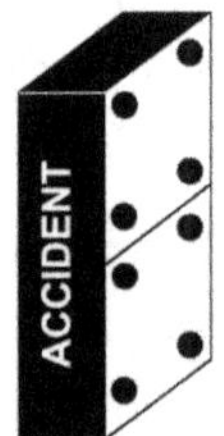

The 5 Factors in an Accident Sequence

Any Injury is Caused by the Action of Preceding Factors

Rather simplistic, perhaps, to modern eyes, it nevertheless clearly demonstrates both problem and solution: Like the childhood game, set up a row of dominoes and tip the first one over, the rest fall unstoppably in sequence. We cannot control our workers' upbringing or attitudes. Still, we can interrupt the fall by controlling what we can—their behavior while on the job and the presence of safety equipment. Remove the center domino, says Heinrich, and the problems never happen.

Real-World Scenarios

Scenario 32: Deepwater Horizon

Deepwater Horizon was a deepwater offshore drilling rig operated by British Petroleum in the Gulf of Mexico. On April 20, 2010, a blowout caused an explosion on the rig that killed 11 crewmen and ignited a fireball visible from 40 miles away. The fire was inextinguishable, and two days later, on April 22, the Horizon collapsed, leaving the well gushing at the seabed, which became the largest marine oil spill in history.

The disaster resulted from a series of safety and management failures. Poor maintenance, inadequate safety systems, and a rushed drilling schedule created a perfect storm. By admitting these smaller issues existed and addressing them early on, BP could've prevented this environmental catastrophe.

Scenario 33: Boeing 737 Crashes

Ethiopian Airlines Flight 302 flew regularly from Addis Ababa, Ethiopia, to Nairobi, Kenya. On March 10, 2019, the Boeing 737 crashed six minutes after takeoff. Lion Air Flight 610 flew from Tangerang to Pangkal Pinang, both in Indonesia. On October 29, 2018, the plane crashed 13 minutes after takeoff. Over 330 passengers and crew members lost their lives on these flights.

The crashes were linked to the aircraft's MCAS software system. Initial design flaws and insufficient pilot training were minor issues that could've been easily corrected but were not. They compounded, leading to tragic outcomes.

Striking the Balance

Vigilance and perfectionism are not enemy combatants. They can and should form a partnership in effective crisis management:

1. Encourage a Culture of Continuous Improvement

Foster an environment where employees feel safe to report minor incidents and near-misses without retribution. Use these reports to identify patterns and areas for improvement.

2. Prioritize Issues Based on Risk

Not all minor issues will lead to crisis. Implement a risk assessment process to prioritize which problems need immediate attention and which can be monitored over time using tools like the Eisenhower Diagram.

3. Invest in Training

Without the skillset, employees can't recognize potential issues early, nor can they address them. Regular training sessions also remind employees to use their situational awareness effectively.

4. Implement Monitoring Systems

Monitoring technology is readily available and constantly improving. Situational awareness includes seeing your environment, work processes and systems, and your equipment continuously. Early detection prevents escalation.

5. Promote Open Communication

Ensure that communication channels are open and effective across all levels of the organization. Encourage personnel to ask questions about situations when they're unsure, to report anything that seems out of place, and to offer suggestions for improvement.

6. Avoid Overburdening

Goals and KPIs should demand that your employees flex and strengthen their muscles, physical or mental, but not to snap them like an overextended rubber band. Strive for excellence, not fantasies. Overburdening leads to burnout, missed details, and increased risk of error instead of decreased risk.

Using KPIs to Detect and Measure Minor Incidents

Implementing solid KPIs can detect minor incidents before they escalate. Suitable KPIs might include:

1. Incident Frequency Rate

Track the number of minor incidents reported over specific periods. A rising trend indicates underlying issues.

2. Near-Miss Reporting Rate

High rates signify a proactive safety culture of people identifying and dealing with potential hazards early.

3. Time to Incident Resolution

Monitor the average time taken to resolve minor incidents. Rapid resolution prevents escalation and demonstrates efficient management.

4. Root Cause Analysis Completion Rate

Regularly and thoroughly analyze the root causes of small incidents. Like a forest fire, if you think you put it out but leave burning embers, you may find yourself dealing with a whole new problem.

5. Employee Training and Awareness Level

Assess the percentage of employees who have completed relevant training. Repeat training on a regular (at a minimum, on an annual) basis.

Integrating these KPIs into your performance metrics creates a robust system where early detection and resolution are always on their minds. A proactive approach mitigates risks and fosters a culture of continuous improvement.

In the Real World

Can you guarantee that this or any crisis will never be repeated? As much as we might wish it, no.

The world spins on, and we spin with it. Sometimes, that spin is dizzying. We can only do the best we can with what each day brings us, but we should always remember:

> There are three types of people in the world:
> Those who make things happen.
> Those who watch things happen.
> Those who wonder, "What happened?"
>
> — Old Proverb

Be the type that makes things happen!

Chapter 7

Tailor the Cure to the Moments

"Keep a Weather Eye Out"

Sailors (from whom that adage comes) lived and died by the weather. The crow's nest wasn't just a place to watch for pirates or enemy ships; the watch was also on the lookout for storms on the horizon. In today's business world, that maritime advice bears frequent repeating: ***You must keep a constant watch.***

Even with due diligence, the situation can pass out of your control. Once it has, you must regain control through an effective response. Some crises come and go in a few minutes or hours—an earthquake or a fire—while others evolve over days, weeks, or months—a political campaign or an economic upheaval. Your response may have to be immediate—to the mall shooter—but it usually evolves with the situation.

These are the moments of duress. Moments where clarity is obscured and where emotions run high. Yet, as daunting as these moments might appear, even the stormiest seas can be navigated with certainty with the right approach. There are countless situations in our lives that surprise us; the unexpected hits us.

In most cases, the surprise is just that, a surprise. However, some unexpected situations have the potential to develop into crises. If you ignore the signs, a crisis may unfold over weeks and months; in other cases, the crisis develops in a split second.

For example, in the story from Chapter 5, the flood—which the car manufacturers couldn't control—temporarily closed the factory that makes a special alloy. Car manufacturers found a temporary manufacturer for their alloy at a factory in another country, and trains were used to carry the raw materials to alternate locations and back—a process that was controllable by car manufacturers.

Suppose, however, that a train strike hit France at the same time—again, uncontrollable by the car manufacturers. With the trains temporarily out of business and material needing to be moved, the car manufacturers would've needed to find some trucks, get them to the right place, off-load the material from the trains or storage areas, and get them rolling—again, this was completely under the car manufacturers control.

Question: Does a nationwide train strike usually happen quietly? Answer: No, the threat of a big strike tends to make the news, and that story develops as the companies and their workers negotiate. If you have a regular transportation need, you must constantly watch the transportation industry.

As soon as the flood struck, while the car manufacturers were arranging a temporary factory and temporary transport, they should also have arranged alternatives for that manufacturing and transport.

The theory is just that simple. Carrying it out effectively is where we separate success from failure.

Obligations Go Both Ways

The train strike was a theoretical example, but something along these lines actually happened:

I worked with a company that had a very serious situation. Their crisis, sadly, ended with them filing for bankruptcy. At some point in the process, a bank employee said, "Ah, don't forget, you have major auto manufacturers as customers. Maybe you should inform them that you've closed the company."

We were able to broker a deal with the car manufacturers for that now-bankrupt company to continue operations for a couple of months. That gave the car manufacturers time to find a new supplier, and it gave some of the employees a couple of extra months to find new jobs without losing paychecks.

In addition to monitoring your stakeholders for things that could positively or negatively affect you, you have a moral obligation to inform them of your situation. I wrote about this earlier. Sometimes, you want to keep your problems hidden if you can solve them before they cause collateral damage, like loss of reputation. It's worth reminding you that your reputation would suffer far more if your company failed to meet its obligations. You caused crises in other companies by keeping intelligence from your stakeholders until it was too late for them to do anything about it. Depending on the details of the situation, keeping things hidden might even open you to very unpleasant legal action.

Tracking Effectiveness of Action Plans

Key Performance Indicators (KPIs)

> Key Performance Indicators (KPIs) are the critical (key) quantifiable indicators of progress toward an intended result. KPIs provide a focus for strategic and operational improvement, create an analytical basis for decision making, and help focus attention on what matters most.
>
> —KPI.org[22]

In both theoretical and actual situations, my companies use KPIs to monitor and improve performance.

Strategic KPIs

Also called "the bird's eye view,"; "the 10,000-foot view," or "the big picture," these KPIs are the broad strokes often used by executives. They may include overall income and profit for a year, employee retention,

[22] Unbylined, "What is a Key Performance Indicator (KPI)?" *KPI.org*. Cary, NC: Strategy Management Group, undated. https://www.kpi.org/KPI-Basics/, accessed August 20, 2024.

total projects completed, or any of a hundred other measurements, depending on the individual company goals.

Tactical KPIs

These are the month-to-month or week-to-week measures or the office-by-office measures. Managers and supervisors analyze shop output, quality, and sales by individual salespeople. These are derived from the company's strategic goals.

Departmental KPIs

Obviously, the sales department is proactive; they go out and bring in new business, while the finance department is mostly reactive. They track what the company or office has spent against what they should've spent. Publicity is both; they create media content and track responses thereto. Some departments will interact with many others; some will operate almost as a company-within-a-company. The KPIs will reflect these differences.

KPI Pros and Cons

Pros	Cons
Help inform management of specific problems and hold employees accountable with quantitative data instead of qualitative data.	Can be "gamed"—supervisors, managers, and even executives can focus on positives and bury negatives unfavorable to them.
Provide quantifiable information useful in strategic planning.	Might require years to collect sufficient data to provide useful intelligence.
Provide clear, specific data on each project or goal.	Can overload workers with too much data or by trying to measure anything, everything, or the wrong things.
Help companies monitor progress toward objectives.	Without constant monitoring and analysis, the intelligence value drops significantly.

Effective Measures

Your KPIs should be tied to your goals and follow the proven standards for effective goal setting: Make them specific, measurable, attainable (but only with real effort), realistically possible, and calendar-based. For example:

The goal, "Grow total revenue by eight percent over last year," might lead to KPIs of:

- Increasing revenue by one percent in the first quarter.
- Two percent each in the second and third quarters.
- Three percent in the fourth.

The goal, "Reduce product returns by 25 percent over the next two years," might lead to KPIs of:

- Increasing quality control inspections by 25 percent.
- Provide continuing education for half the shop staff this year and half next year.
- Conduct an engineering review of each component to improve the design.

KPIs need to be stated simply and clearly so that each employee understands them and can tell you how their function contributes to each KPI. (Each job will contribute to one or two; at least, only a few will contribute to all the company's goals.)

KPIs are the beginning of a plan. If you want to increase sales, you might plan to attend more trade shows or conventions; you might increase your presence or number of salespeople attending a trade show or your presence on social media. If you want to retrain your shop jockeys, you'll need to find training opportunities and create a schedule of who goes where and when.

Write KPIs in Pencil

Like any aspect of business, KPIs may need to change as your situation changes. If your sales staff achieves their goal of increasing by seven percent in July, maybe you'll want a more ambitious goal. If someone finds a flaw and corrects it, reducing returns by 12 percent, you might want to challenge the shop jockeys to go for a 30 percent drop instead of 25 percent.

As businesses grow, they have more staff, more projects, more money, and more problems to deal with. Overloading people with too many KPIs will become counter-productive. People can only focus on so many things at a time. Set some KPIs as high priority; the rest as low priority using an Eisenhower Diagram or other tool.[23]

Monitoring and Controlling

As soon as you have a crisis response action plan (AP), you need, of course, to continuously monitor and evaluate the effectiveness of the AP. This is the only way to ensure that (1) the AP is carried out as written, (2) you're producing the results that you need, and (3) you can adjust the AP if necessary. We use several monitoring methods in real-time, tracking implementation as it occurs.

This includes, for example, operational monitoring, in which we keep track of all the resources deployed. In a manufacturing setting, we'd track parts produced, parts delivered, parts not produced because you lacked raw materials, and so on. Every part then becomes part (no pun intended) of a database. Side by side with production, we track quality inspections and issues.

We also track the transportation needed to deliver the product to customers, adjusting our transport methods to meet the challenges of the crisis. On some occasions, that has included shipping air freight (fast and expensive) instead of ground (slow and cheap). In one very-high-priority matter, helicopter flights went straight from the factory's parking lot to the customer's parking lot. Those helicopters carried just enough essential parts to ensure that an assembly line in a car manufacturer's facility kept running for, as I recall, the two hours we needed to ship the rest of the parts by truck. That's an expensive proposition, but in that instance, it is less expensive than shutting down an entire auto assembly line for a couple of hours.

[23] This section derived from Alexandra Twin, "KPIs: What Are Key Performance Indicators? Types and Examples," Investopedia.com, January 30, 2024. New York City: Dotdash Meredith, https://www.investopedia.com/terms/k/kpi.asp, accessed August 20, 2024, and Unbylined, "What is a KPI?" Qlik.com. King of Prussia, PA: Qlik Technologies Inc., undated. https://www.qlik.com/us/kpi, accessed August 20, 2024.

Cost versus benefit must be tracked in every crisis. Budget is a KPI, and remember, ***there's no profit in crisis management; it's all about limiting losses***. So, I think we spent $15,000 on that helicopter operation. By the way, people are going to ask questions when you spend that kind of money. You'll need good answers to those questions. In that case, the question is, "Exactly how much would it cost to shut down the assembly line for two hours?" (I won't say, but it was a lot more than $15,000!)

That leads to monitoring communications. In the helicopter incident, we were in constant touch with the trucks, making sure they'd arrive on time. In general terms, we frequently assess the effectiveness of communication channels within an organization. In larger companies, you often have an intranet to link executives with employees and other stakeholders, and, of course, the internet can connect you to the press, government agencies, and others.

Feedback Loops

How do we create feedback loops? The easy way is to ask the stakeholders, "How are we doing?"

It's very much like the OODA Loop—Observe, Orient, Decide, and Act. It promotes rapid responses, processed in real-time—sometimes, right in the thick of the action. You can ask for feedback by comparing real-time info with the action plan and adjusting the plan on the spot when necessary.

In addition to direct questioning, during which some people hesitate to be honest, these modern times provide huge amounts of open-source intelligence (OSINT) available to everybody for monitoring trends in real time. This works best when you have a large number of customers or employees affected by a crisis of confidence. It may sound silly to ask, "What's trending on Facebook and Instagram about this or that?" "What hashtags might be about you?"

In past generations, one might hear, "His life is an open book," meaning he's one who keeps no secrets about himself. Well, people today, especially the younger generations, are open books, often giving up dangerous amounts of info on social media. It takes time to dig through all the posts, tweets, chats, and whatever else they call them, but social media is a valuable OSINT tool for certain situations. In operational monitoring, if your company has the right setup, you can obtain OSINT results simply by pushing a few buttons and activating your existing IT system.

Even your machines, most of which are computer-controlled these days, can be configured to report important data to a central workstation. There, you can read up-to-the-minute details on output, downtimes, who was operating the machine on each shift, and more.

If you don't have these sophisticated, automated, latest bells-and-whistles tools, go old school. Task a member of the crisis management team, the one who's compiling all the data, to walk around with a notebook or with his phone's camera/video recorder, asking questions, making notes, taking photos, making videos, and generally tracking or checking on everything.

This, you might recall, is not OSINT; it's HUMINT—human intelligence. Despite all our advancements in technology, sometimes you need face-to-face personal contact to get the information you need. Never underestimate the capability of "boots on the ground," as we said in the military, or of using the old "mark-1 eyeball."

Good Manners

In nation-to-nation espionage, there are few rules. The action plan usually involves clandestine operations where the opposition never knew you were there. It's one of the keys to earning a pension and being around long enough to collect it. In business, we avoid such things, as governments tend to frown on industrial espionage.

Of course, sometimes external stakeholders have useful knowledge we'll need to be most effective in mitigating and preventing crises. In such cases, there are protocols and courtesies when obtaining HUMINT. If obtaining HUMINT involves high-level management, one tread lightly. The CEO or some other high-level executive or leader needs to make the initial contact with his/her counterpart, ask for their cooperation, and, perhaps, even be the one to conduct the interview.

Even an internal crisis management team needs to move carefully. There are laws protecting employee privacy, protecting against hostile work environments, and so on. Before we set up interviews with employees, we make upper echelons aware of the plan and let them oversee its execution. Who will be interviewed? What questions will we ask? If the employees are unionized, will a union representative be attending interviews? If legal responsibility for any damage or injury is up for discussion, employees may have the right (or, depending on the situation, you might encourage them) to have legal counsel present during all interviews.

This is something I haven't yet discussed and could be the subject of a fairly long book if some lawyer hasn't already written one. Whenever the subject of fault arises, crisis managers have the obligation to respect and protect the rights of anyone who potentially, could be found at fault. As crisis managers, internal or consultant, we're not the police nor the courts. We have our function, they have theirs, and we respect their needs as we hope they respect ours.

On the Front Lines

Something else that people rarely think about, unless they're politicians running for re-election: Whether the crisis is confined to a building or a small town or covers a wide area of a state, ***go there*** as quickly as practical. See the situation for yourself or as much of it as possible. Utilize that mark-1 eyeball, the audio and video recorder in your phone, and whatever other intelligence gathering equipment you can take with you.

Neither the media nor official sources will tell you everything. Government agencies and law enforcement, in particular, probably don't even want you to ask. That takes resources away from their crisis management activities. That doesn't mean you should not monitor their public statements; just don't accept them as full and complete details of the crisis.

Where a location is a crime scene or has suffered damage due to an earthquake, fire, or some other major disaster, stay away. You can't help in the early stages, and you'd probably be in the way of people who can help. Only after the situation stabilizes and you can be in the area without risking yourself or others is the time for an onsite visit.

In less newsworthy situations, such as our ongoing example of a major customer not paying their bills for some reason, you should definitely get on site and see it for yourself—as soon as you know there's a crisis in progress, if possible. Maybe you'll learn nothing; a company in crisis often wants to keep everything out of the public eye as long as it can. Then again, they may be very grateful to see you arrive and ask, "How can I help?"

By the way, I mentioned that intelligence gathering isn't always viewed as ethical. Here's a dilemma for you to consider:

The timing and purpose of your visit will depend on the situation. In Chapter 3, I mentioned a restaurant that told its food supplier it couldn't pay its bill. In such a case, I would invoke the aforementioned "First Rule of Journalism—Trust but verify." I might invite a half-dozen employees to visit that restaurant at lunch or dinner, at company expense, to gather intelligence. The responses might include:

"No wonder they can't pay their bills; the service is lousy, and the food is worse."

"The food is great. The waitress was adorable, but the place was empty."

"I can't imagine why they're having money troubles. It was so crowded we had to wait half an hour to be seated."

What would you do if you got any of those responses from your intel gatherers?

Learning by Sad Experience

Experience shows that it generally takes the same amount of time to get out of a crisis as it took for the crisis to develop.

That's not a hard-and-fast rule; natural disasters tend to strike swiftly and, often, without warning. In business, personal, or governmental crises, however, things move more slowly. This is the best time to tailor the cure to the moment. If you can recognize an impending doom, you might mitigate much of it; you might even solve the crisis while it's still in the problem or annoyance stage of gestation.

The After-Action Report

When all is said and done, at least sufficiently that you can relax and take stock, an after-action report (AAR) becomes the official record of the crisis and your response. It can be a vital tool in your long-term strategy to prevent a repeat of the crisis. The AAR answers two basic questions: What Went Right? What Went Wrong? It's also the demonstration of transparency—we don't want any lawyers thinking we are hiding anything, do we? How do you go about documenting those successes and failures?

The AAR is the result of serious reflection on what happened during the crisis: The author will use the 5 Whys, the questions of journalism, OSINT, HUMINT, and everything we've talked about to create a written document covering every aspect of the situation. It needs to be done in a structured way and, again, if you don't have someone in the organization with the skills to put the data together so that it cannot be misunderstood, consider hiring an outside talent to craft the report:

1. AARs begin by describing the crisis and how it came about.
2. AARs list the crisis management team, how the team was formed, who was in-house and who was outside talent, what role each member played, the strengths and weaknesses of each, and the level of team cohesion.
3. AARs describe the course of action, the action plan, the timeline, and all the KPIs.
4. AARS summarizes interviews with key stakeholders—owners, managers, shop jockeys, certainly vendors, clients, government agencies, or the media possibly—detailing how they feel things went from their perspective.
5. AARs identify successes and shortcomings, how the AP failed and was adjusted, if all KPIs were met, and why or why not.
6. AARs detail the budget and how it was determined and spent; did the crisis management team overspend or come in under budget?
7. AARs recommend actions to prevent future crises of this type.

All the intelligence collected during the crisis and the aftermath is the raw data from which the AAR will be synthesized. It will include those critical-to-understand items, the effectiveness of the mitigation plan, and the decisions made during the event.

Once again, legal issues arise. Admitting fault potentially opens one up to legal reprisal. However, if government agencies are involved, hiding any facts can open one up to criminal charges.

Every step of the way, from the recognition of a pending or existing crisis to the publication of the after-action report, involves decisions—hundreds, maybe thousands of them. When you see a better way, don't hesitate to make that decision and change course. That's one of the things you're getting paid to do.

Appendix 1

Special Cases

This book is about the general principles of crisis management. To conclude, I've added the following articles on two specific areas that should be of real concern to most businesses.

"Risk Management in a Nutshell—Where Do I Begin?"

We're Always Hungry for Success

Risk management is a critical component of daily life and, of course, running any business, regardless of its size or industry. It involves anticipating potential challenges and implementing strategies to prevent or mitigate their impact.

While risk management can seem daunting, as someone specializing in risk management for the automotive industry, I've found it revolves around four basic strategies: avoidance, reduction, transfer, and acceptance. These strategies are universal, and, in my experience, every decision about managing risk falls into one of these categories. For the purposes of this article, the examples below are simplified, so keep in mind that in the real world, such decisions require a thorough assessment of your specific situation.

Four Basic Strategies to Cope with Risk

1. Avoidance

Avoidance involves taking steps to completely eliminate the risk. This strategy involves making decisions that steer you clear of potential dangers altogether. However, it's important to note that while avoidance is the most effective way to prevent negative outcomes, it often means forgoing opportunities with inherent risks.

Example: A software company is considering entering a market known for its strict and frequently changing regulations. The potential legal complications and costs associated with compliance are high. By deciding not to enter this market, the company avoids these risks altogether.

2. Reduction

Reduction focuses on minimizing either the likelihood or the impact of the risk. Unlike avoidance, which eliminates the risk, reduction involves taking actions that reduce the chances of the risk materializing or lessening its effects if it does.

Example: A manufacturing company is concerned about workplace injuries. Instead of avoiding the manufacturing process altogether, which is not feasible, the company implements safety training programs, installs protective gear, and regularly maintains equipment to reduce the risk of accidents.

3. Transfer

Transferring the risk involves shifting the risk to another party. This is often done through contracts or insurance. This strategy doesn't eliminate the risk but rather moves the financial burden or responsibility for managing it to another entity.

Example: A retail business that operates in multiple locations might purchase insurance to cover potential damages from natural disasters like floods or earthquakes. In doing so, the financial risk associated with these events is transferred to the insurance company.

4. Acceptance

Acceptance involves acknowledging the risk and choosing to bear the consequences if it occurs. This approach is often used when the cost of avoiding, reducing, or transferring the risk outweighs the potential impact of the risk itself.

Example: A startup launching a new product might recognize the risk of low initial sales due to limited brand recognition. Instead of spending heavily on marketing to avoid this risk, the company might accept it, understanding that slow sales are a part of its growth strategy.

How to Start With Risk Management in Your Organization

If you're new to risk management or uncertain about how to implement it in your organization, it's best to start small and gradually expand. Begin by focusing on the areas you directly manage—whether that's a department, project, or a particular segment of the business.

1. Identify and List the Risks

First, you'll need to identify the risks that could impact your department or project, including financial, operational, strategic, or external risks like market changes. Engage your entire team in this process to ensure you capture a broad range of potential issues.

To identify risks effectively, I often suggest starting by asking your team, "What could potentially go wrong at each phase of this project?" and "Are there any external factors that might disrupt our operations?" Another useful approach is conducting a SWOT analysis, which involves identifying strengths, weaknesses, opportunities, and threats. This exercise can help bring to light both internal and external risks that might not be immediately obvious but could impact your project or department.

2. Evaluate the Risks

Once risks are identified, determine how likely those risks are to occur and how they could impact your objectives. Then, prioritize risks based on these factors. In doing so, you can focus your efforts on managing the most significant threats.

When it comes to evaluating risks, one best practice is to use a risk matrix. This tool helps you assess the likelihood and the potential impact of each risk so that you can prioritize them accordingly. I also recommend involving a cross-functional team in the evaluation process. These team members can provide different perspectives, which leads to a more accurate assessment of the risks and their potential consequences.

3. Assign Each Risk to a Strategy

After evaluating the risks, assign each risk to one of the four risk management strategies: avoidance, reduction, transfer, or acceptance. Remember, you can only apply one strategy to each risk. Choosing the strategy for each specific risk involves considering three key factors:

- The severity of the potential impact.
- The cost and feasibility of mitigation.
- How much risk the organization is willing to tolerate.

For example, if a risk could significantly disrupt operations but is too expensive to avoid or transfer, reducing the risk might be the best course of action. Conversely, smaller risks with less impact might be better handled by simply accepting them.

By applying these strategies, you can manage risks effectively in any part of your organization. Remember, each situation is unique, and the best strategy will depend on a careful assessment of the specific circumstances and potential impacts of the risks your team is facing. As you become more familiar with these strategies, you'll likely find that risk management becomes a natural part of your decision-making process. As a result, you can steer your organization through uncertainties with greater confidence.

"Riding the Wave of Uncertainty"

Risk Mitigation Strategies for Supply Chain Disruptions

In an era where disruption is the new normal, supply chain resilience is no longer an option; it's a critical requirement. Global events, ranging from trade wars to pandemics to military conflicts, have highlighted the fragility of our global supply chains. Ensuring their reliability in these uncertain times is a challenge every business must confront. The essence of tackling this challenge lies in identifying vulnerabilities and implementing risk prevention strategies:

1. Map out your entire supply chain from raw materials to end users—yes, transportation from your factory to the retail outlet is part of your supply chain. (They can't buy it unless you get it in front of them.)
2. Conduct thorough risk assessments on each link of the chain.
3. Implement rigorous prevention strategies—including alternative sources, natural and manufactured disasters, political upheaval, and whatever you have nightmares about.

I recommend the following strategies:

1. Diversification

The old adage of not putting all your eggs in one basket remains a potent metaphor today. In the past, businesses primarily focused on costs and available capacity. Today, it's shifted toward ensuring the reliability of raw materials and components by diversifying suppliers. Sourcing from a single region or supplier leaves you vulnerable to the smallest disruption. Multiple suppliers and logistical partners across different geographical locations increase the resilience of your supply chain.

2. Digital Transformation

Incorporating advanced analytics, AI, and machine learning can provide your business with increased predictive insights, enabling you to anticipate disruptions and take proactive measures. Predictive analytics can leverage historical data to detect patterns, forecast trends or outcomes, and even predict future demand.

Technologies like the Internet of Things (IoT) can enhance transparency, providing real-time visibility into supply chain operations and accelerating response times. IoT systems provide real-time tracking during transit and environmental monitoring for temperature-sensitive items. Warehouse management tech also helps ensure optimal storage conditions and efficient logistics.

3. Strong Supplier Relationships

Cultivating strong relationships with suppliers contributes to a more collaborative and resilient supply chain. Mutual trust and understanding lead to better communication, problem-solving, and shared risk management. It also allows for added flexibility and adaptability in responding to disruptions. For example:

- Investing in your suppliers through training or technology helps ensure that they grow with you.
- Regular check-ins, feedback loops, and open forums among stakeholders foster a culture of transparency and trust.
- Collaboration on business goals, objectives, and plans helps ensure that both parties benefit from the relationship.

4. Adopting a "Just-In-Time" (JIT) Approach

Companies employ the JIT approach to increase efficiency and decrease waste by receiving goods precisely when they're needed, reducing inventory costs. However, JIT can leave businesses vulnerable—exposed to disruptions because they have a minimal inventory stockpile.

5. Updating Risk Mitigation Plans

Risk management is not a one-time process. Plans must be reviewed and updated regularly to ensure they stay relevant and at peak effectiveness. Conduct regular planning exercises (like wargames) to prepare your business for a variety of disruptions. The scenarios should reflect a range of crises, from minor local disruptions to major global events. These exercises allow employees to identify potential weak points in their supply chain and develop contingency plans.

Regardless of the enterprise's size, management must be focused on this issue. I recommend appointing a dedicated manager over risk management tasks. Employees should also be trained in basic risk management and mitigation strategies, as they may well form the first line of defense.

6. Conclusion

Navigating the complexity of modern supply chains is challenging. Disruptions are inevitable but disaster for you is not. Disruption effects can be reduced, sometimes avoided, through careful planning and efficient execution. Create a resilient supply chain, and your company will bounce back stronger.

"The Human Factor in Cyber-Risk"

Training and Culture as Defense Mechanisms

Cybersecurity is not just a technological battleground; it's a human arena. As organizations deploy sophisticated defenses against cyber threats, attackers continually refine their tactics to exploit more vulnerable targets—you and me.

Email attachments can contain viruses and spyware, while phishing messages exploit human vulnerabilities, bypassing even the most sophisticated defenses; the list of potential assaults on your privacy and property is long and frightening. Effective training programs and a robust security culture are essential in fortifying a company's defense against cyberattacks.

In my role managing risk and crises for Fortune 500 companies, I've seen firsthand how a single human click can unravel months of cybersecurity preparation. Recently, we were deployed to assist two companies experiencing severe disruptions in their supply chains. The root cause of each was a cyberattack. I fear that, despite our best efforts, both companies will have to file for bankruptcy.

We Can Mitigate the Risk of Such Attacks

Cybersecurity training is indispensable. Unfortunately, it's often underutilized or overlooked. To strengthen human factors, organizations must first assess their existing training programs. Once cybersecurity status has been assessed, you can then design training programs to fill in existing gaps or weaknesses. These programs need to be dynamic and mirror real-world scenarios to keep employees engaged. Interactive simulations and game-style learning experiences are popular and can greatly improve effectiveness and information retention.

For example, simulated phishing exercises not only teach employees how to identify potential threats but also offer practical, hands-on experience. Consistent training for all employees keeps them sharp and helps maintain their situational awareness. Truly effective training instills in people a healthy dose of skepticism: Do you really know that person requesting a connection on social media?

Building a Robust Security Culture

Corporate culture gently pushes employees to continually work in specific ways that advance the company's goals. It surpasses mere policies and procedures; it instills attitudes, behaviors, and values shared across the company regarding cybersecurity and other matters.

Building a culture starts with understanding that it encompasses participation at all levels, from the shop floor to the C-suite. Its key objective, striking a balance between healthy skepticism and enhanced awareness, enables employees to identify and question the red flags that indicate threats.

Leadership plays a pivotal role in cultivating a security-first mindset. Executives must demonstrate their commitment through actions like participating in training sessions alongside lower-echelon employees. This sends a clear message that cybersecurity is a priority at all levels of the organization.

Preventing Cyber-Extortion

One of the more sinister forms of cyberattacks involves extortion—attackers threatening to release sensitive information unless their demands are met. Educating employees about such threats is the crucial first step in prevention. Training should detail what types of information might be targeted and the tactics they employ, such as phishing emails or social engineering attacks.

Encouraging open communication across the organization is vital. Employees must feel comfortable reporting any suspicious activity without fear of reprisal or judgment. This open dialogue can often stop cyber threats in their tracks before they escalate.

Moreover, a comprehensive incident response plan should be in place to address potential extortion situations. This plan should include steps for containing the breach, assessing the damage, and communicating, internally and externally, with the legal department, law enforcement, and psychological support for victims.

Avoiding Real-Life Industrial Espionage

Industrial espionage has always been a problem, but advancing technology simply makes it easier—for the bad guys.

Attackers determine what specific information they need and identify a target who can provide it. For example, they might target a car manufacturer to steal research data on new fuel cells. Using social media, attackers can gather information about the target company's employees. They may create fake profiles on social media, posing as recruiters or industry professionals to connect with employees and gain their trust.

Next, attackers develop tailored social engineering schemes. This might involve crafting phishing emails that appear to come from a trusted source or engaging in conversation to extract sensitive information using fake social media profiles. The stolen information can then be shared with a competing business or a state actor.

Several countries have extensive anti-cyberattack programs. Businesses can learn from these programs—how to stay informed on the latest threats, the need for continuous employee education, and the value of proactive engagement with cybersecurity experts.

Appendix 2

Quick Reference Guide

The Crisis

If someone comes to kill you, rise up and kill him first.
—The Babylonian Talmud

Definition

A crisis exists any time that your circumstances pass beyond your control. Your priority must be to regain control.

Crises arise all over the world every day. Most will never touch you noticeably. When they do, you must act.

Response

Most animals run at the sight of lions because few animals can win against a lion.

We see disasters as lions, unstoppably deadly. We see ourselves as prey.

Look to mythology: Dragons, creatures of immense size and strength, represent the unstoppable force.

Become the dragon!

Paradigm

There are billions of things I can't control in the world. There is one thing I can always control—***me***.

1. Get a Grip, Keep a Grip

> If you can solve your problem, then what is the need of worrying? If you cannot solve it, then what is the use of worrying?
>
> —Shantideva

2. Keep it Simple

> The simplest explanation is usually the best one.
>
> —Ockham's Razor

3. Act Decisively

> A good solution applied with vigor now is better than a perfect solution applied ten minutes later.
>
> —George Smith Patton, Jr.

4. Be Unstoppable

> Never give in. Never give in. … Never yield to the apparently overwhelming might of the enemy.
>
> —Sir Winston Churchill

5. End the Threat

> It ain't over till it's ***over***.
>
> —Lawrence Peter "Yogi" Berra (emphasis added)

The Schwenk Cycle
"Admit then A.D.M.I.T."

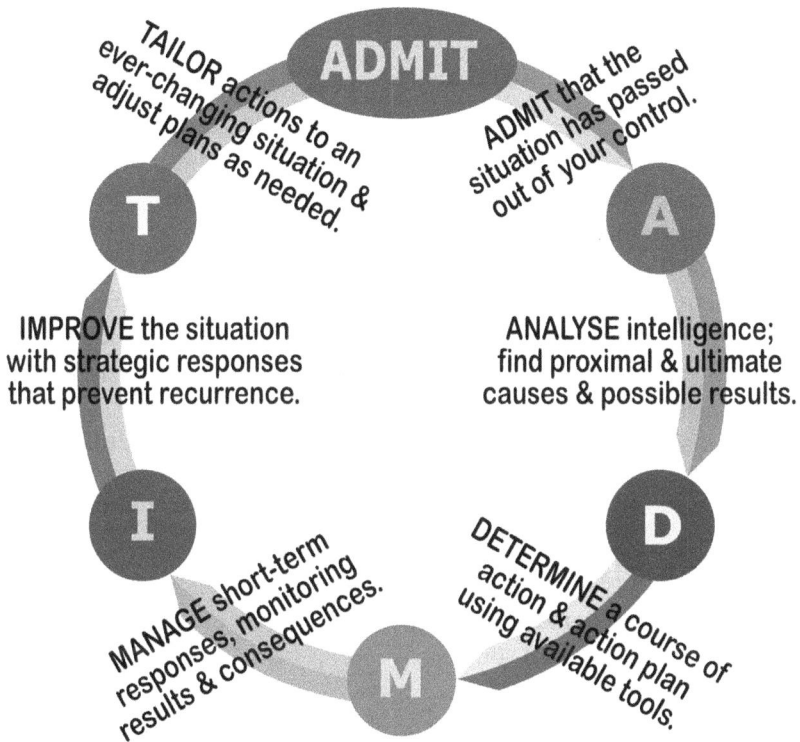

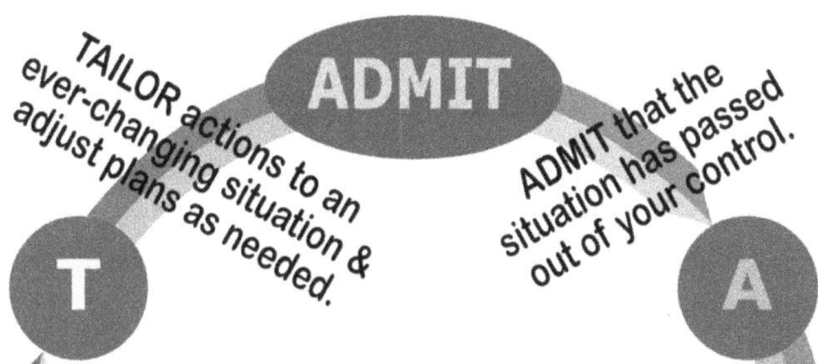

ADMIT
ADMIT that the situation has passed out of your control.
A
TAILOR actions to an ever-changing situation & adjust plans as needed.
T

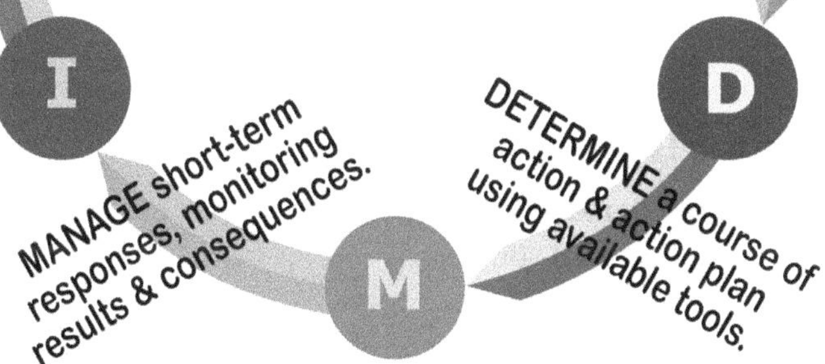

ANALYSE intelligence; find proximal & ultimate causes & possible results.

DETERMINE a course of action & action plan using available tools.

MANAGE short-term responses, monitoring results & consequences.

Our Purpose:

1. To provide individuals & businesses with a clear, actionable framework to effectively manage crises.
2. To equip all parties with practical tools & methods needed to navigate unexpected situations & emerge stronger.

The Schwenk Cycle

Anytime your situation has passed out of your control, you are in a crisis. Pretending it doesn't exist guarantees a result you won't like.

Understand Your Situation

Size—it's better to deal with problems while they're small—an annoyance can easily grow into a crisis.

Paranoia—an old joke reminds us, "Just because you're paranoid doesn't mean that no one's after you."

Honesty—if you can't bring yourself to admit there's a crisis, you can't focus and won't act.

Focus—Deal with what you can control; forget the rest, for now.

Ignorance—crises often arise because someone hasn't asked the right questions or any questions.

Denial—when problems are small, it's easy to pretend they don't exist.

Intelligence Is the Core of the Cycle

Intelligence is actionable information—data you can use to improve your situation. Potential sources:

- **Open-Source Intelligence (OSINT)**—media reports, public databases, web and print publications; anything the public can access without restriction.
- **Social Media Intelligence (SOCMINT)**—anything published on social media platforms—which is a lot!
- **Human Intelligence (HUMINT)**—data gained from human interaction—personal interviews, observation, public forums, trade shows, and even gossip.
- **Geospatial Intelligence (GEOINT)**—data from satellite images, aerial photography (drones), etc.

- **Electronic Intelligence (ELINT)**—voice, data, and other electronic communications—often involves legally protected information, so tread very carefully.

Intelligence Countermeasures

If you are watching them, assume they are watching you. Use all available options to safeguard your data.

The Intelligence Process

1. **Plan and Direct**—define requirements and set objectives.
2. **Collect**—gather raw data from all sources.
3. **Process**—decrypt, translate, sort, and organize.
4. **Analyze**—combine critical thinking with subject expertise to provide context and understanding.
5. **Disseminate**—to those with need-to-know.
6. **Feedback**—evaluate the results for the efficiency of collection and quality of the results.

The Ishikawa Diagram
(ALSO CALLED "THE FISHBONE ANALYSIS")

THE SYMPTOM is not THE PROBLEM.

THE PROBLEM

Find THE SOURCE and you find THE PROBLEM.

Potential sources

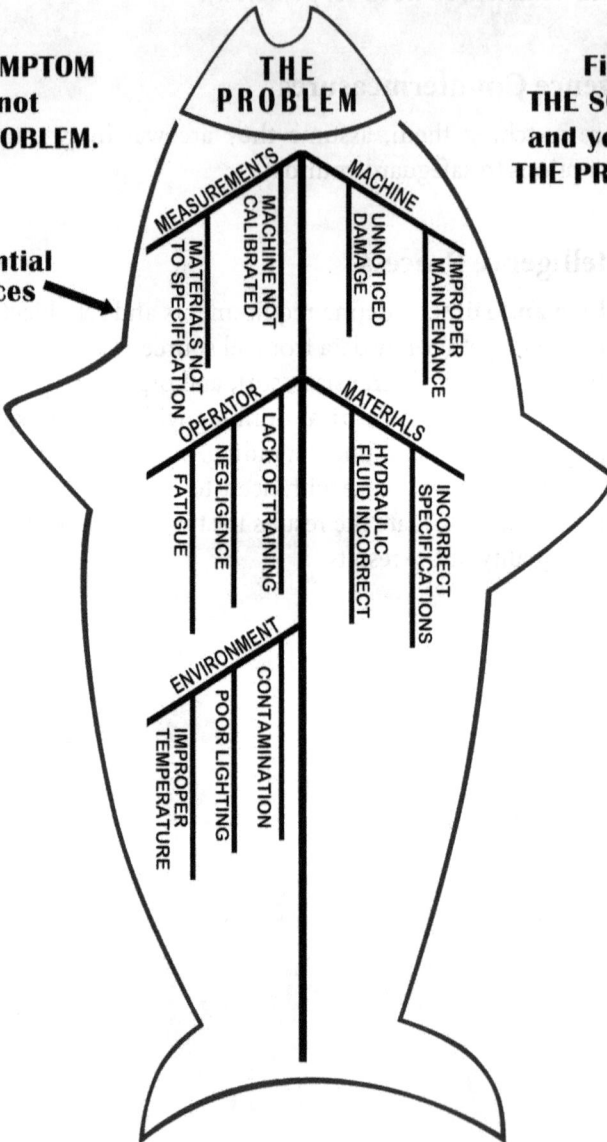

MEASUREMENTS
MACHINE NOT CALIBRATED
MATERIALS NOT TO SPECIFICATION

MACHINE
UNNOTICED DAMAGE
IMPROPER MAINTENANCE

OPERATOR
LACK OF TRAINING
NEGLIGENCE
FATIGUE

MATERIALS
HYDRAULIC FLUID INCORRECT
INCORRECT SPECIFICATIONS

ENVIRONMENT
CONTAMINATION
POOR LIGHTING
IMPROPER TEMPERATURE

THE ISHIKAWA DIAGRAM

It isn't that they can't see the solution. It is that they can't see the problem.

—Gilbert Keith Chesterton

Proximal Cause versus Ultimate Cause

In US law, the ***proximal cause*** of a situation is ***what happened***; the ***ultimate cause*** of a situation is ***why it happened***. It's also called the ***root cause***. That ultimate or root cause is what you need to find before you can firmly and decisively end the crisis. There are several methods.

The "5 Why" Method

You ask why A happened, and you're told, "Because of B."
You ask why B happened, and you're told, "Because of C."
You ask why C happened, and you're told, "Because of D."
You ask why D happened, and you're told, "Because of E."

By the time you get to E, you've probably hit the root cause. All the info collected during this process can be difficult to visualize.

The Ishikawa Diagram

A great tool for organizing your "whys," it turns raw data into an easily understood, relational illustration. Also called "the Fishbone Diagram" (it looks like a fish skeleton), it allows a crisis management team to see the whole picture at a glance—a situation overview.

Risk Assessment

Identify

By asking the five whys, we clarify the root problem. We can eliminate other possible causes not pertaining to this situation—but which should be watched for the prevention of future problems.

Quantify

Once identified, we gauge both the potential impact of problems.

Prioritize

Once quantified, we can deal with the risks carrying the greatest or the most immediate threat, then the others in their turn.

Evaluate

Once prioritized, each risk can be weighed—cost of repair versus replacement of a device, speed of a process against potential for errors, etc. Such assessments ensure that risk management remains in harmony with the long-term objectives.

Mitigate and Manage

Once evaluated, instinctive (short-term) and tactical (mid-term) actions are initiated while considering and eventually implementing strategic (long-term) decisions that prevent recurrences—transferring risks, changing processes, engaging additional safeguards, etc.

Effective Risk Management

Dealing properly with challenges is a dual-edged sword. It safeguards present profits while paving the way for future opportunities, growth, and improvement.

The SWOT Analysis

SWOT is an acronym for **S**trengths, **W**eaknesses, **O**pportunities, and **T**hreats.

If you're not in a crisis at the moment, you aren't necessarily safe.

SWOT sees both internal and external factors.

Identifying strengths and weaknesses is an exercise in knowing yourself, and identifying opportunities and threats is an exercise in watching the world. Both are key elements of situational awareness.

If reviewed regularly and incorporated into discussions of KPIs, tactical and strategic goals, and other business or personal processes, SWOT can assist leaders in developing strategies for most effectively using strengths to:

- Improve on strengths.
- Take advantage of opportunities.
- Address and overcome weaknesses.
- Minimize or eliminate threats.

SWOT in Crisis

When a crisis strikes, your situation changes.

What changes does it bring to each item in your SWOT Matrix?

A swift reassessment provides intelligence that can guide changes in plans and priorities.

SWOT Analyses can be related to the Jochen Matrix, the Ishikawa Diagram, the OODA Loop, and other management tools for more extensive investigation.

Keeping every involved stakeholder "in the loop" can prevent a crisis escalation.

Conducting a SWOT Analysis

1. Designate a facilitator who can keep discussions moving and on an effective path.
2. Designate a recorder to assist the leader; list discussion items on wall charts; take notes on or record all discussions; prepare and distribute minutes.
3. Review the SWOT method and its purpose so that everybody is on the same page. (A review of the organization's vision and mission statements might be helpful here.)
4. Have each participant introduce themself—name, title, department, and responsibilities.

5. If the group is large, divide participants into brainstorming groups—each with a facilitator and recorder—mixing departments to provide a variety of opinions in each group.
6. Instruct the groups to be thorough, encouraging them to avoid ruling out any ideas. (If an idea doesn't work, it can be discarded later.)
7. Once lists have been generated, gather the group together and combine the lists into one large matrix.
8. Discuss and record all results, coming to a consensus on the most important items in each category.
9. Relate the analysis to the organization's vision, mission, and goals.
10. Translate the analysis to courses of action and action plans.
11. Set a time and place to reconvene and review.

THE SWOT ANALYSIS

SWOT enhances your situational awareness and your ability to evaluate your competitive position in your marketplace.

Displays that intelligence in a clear, understandable format.

Displays strengths and opportunities alongside weaknesses and threats, allowing you to judge the true nature of each.

A well-executed SWOT analysis provides fact-based investigation by which you can make better tactical and strategic decisions and inspire new products or markets.

SWOT can assist in: Taking advantage of opportunities.
Addressing and overcoming weaknesses.
Minimizing or eliminating threats.

A small manufacturer's SWOT analysis might look something like this:

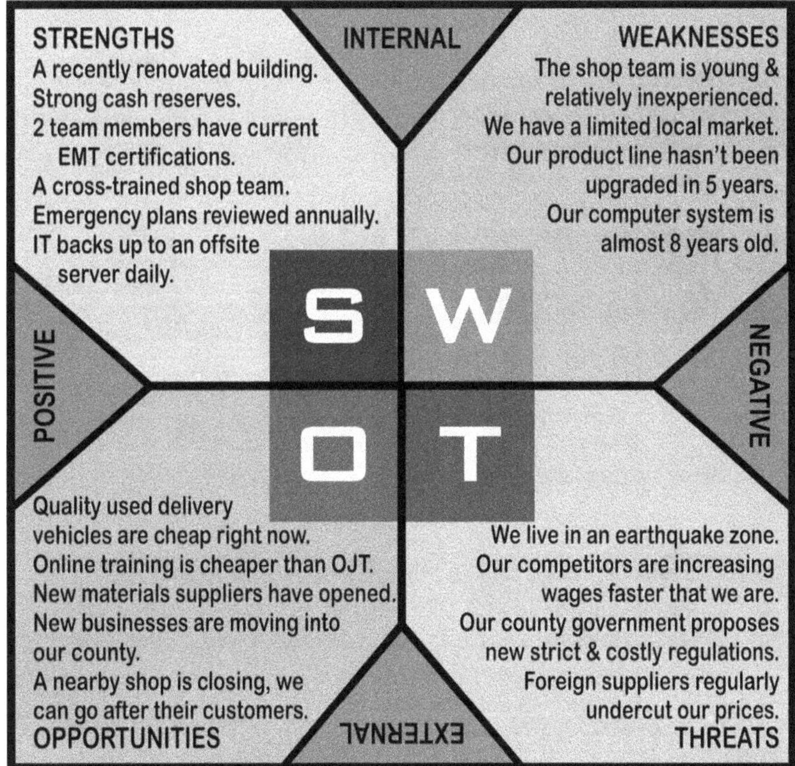
STRENGTHS
A recently renovated building.
Strong cash reserves.
2 team members have current EMT certifications.
A cross-trained shop team.
Emergency plans reviewed annually.
IT backs up to an offsite server daily.
INTERNAL
WEAKNESSES
The shop team is young & relatively inexperienced.
We have a limited local market.
Our product line hasn't been upgraded in 5 years.
Our computer system is almost 8 years old.
S W O T
POSITIVE
NEGATIVE
Quality used delivery vehicles are cheap right now.
Online training is cheaper than OJT.
New materials suppliers have opened.
New businesses are moving into our county.
A nearby shop is closing, we can go after their customers.
OPPORTUNITIES
EXTERNAL
We live in an earthquake zone.
Our competitors are increasing wages faster that we are.
Our county government proposes new strict & costly regulations.
Foreign suppliers regularly undercut our prices.
THREATS

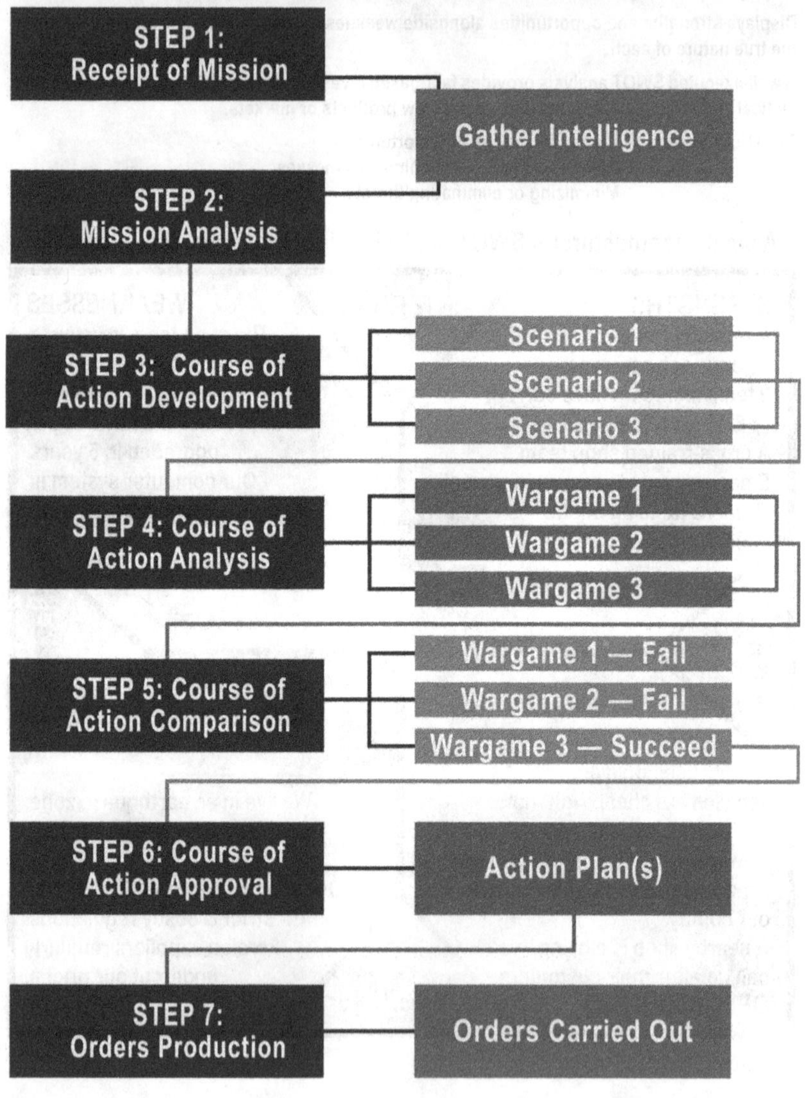
THE MILITARY
DECISION-MAKING PROCESS
(WITH ADDITIONS BY SCHWENK)
STEP 1:
Receipt of Mission
Gather Intelligence
STEP 2:
Mission Analysis
STEP 3: Course of
Action Development
Scenario 1
Scenario 2
Scenario 3
STEP 4: Course of
Action Analysis
Wargame 1
Wargame 2
Wargame 3
STEP 5: Course of
Action Comparison
Wargame 1 — Fail
Wargame 2 — Fail
Wargame 3 — Succeed
STEP 6: Course of
Action Approval
Action Plan(s)
STEP 7:
Orders Production
Orders Carried Out

The Military Decision-Making Process (MDMP)

The Plan

Crisis management planning involves two steps:

- Choosing a "course of action" (COA)—a comprehensive overview of objectives, alternatives, calculated risks and benefits.
- Designing an "action plan" (AP)—a detailed set of tasks required to bring the COA to completion.

Remember

> No battle plan ever survives first contact with the enemy.
>
> —Ancient Military Truism

The idea we call "the butterfly effect" or "the law of unintended consequences" reminds us that we are interconnected, interrelated, and interdependent. "What you don't know can't hurt you" is a fool's paradise. Remain flexible and adjust APs as necessary.

The Process

1. Receipt of Mission

This usually comes from an external source—the root cause of the crisis.

2. Mission Analysis

Gather and analyze intelligence, consider variables, and define a successful outcome.

3. Course of Action (COA) Development

Identify the actions you might take—give yourself at least three options.

4. COA Analysis (aka Wargaming)

Test each potential COAs whenever possible—observe successes, failures, and consequences.

5. COA Comparison

Evaluate the practice outcomes compared to expectations. Choose the best option.

6. COA Approval

Obtain permissions (from owners, senior management, and government agencies) as needed, then create an action plan.

7. Orders Production

Distribute orders and execute the AP. Tell the people what they need to do and get to it!

The CARVER Technique

Criticality — How critical is the asset or site?
Accessibility — How easy would it be to access the site?
Recoverability — How easy would it be for the site to recover from an attack?
Vulnerability — How vulnerable is the target to an attack?
Effect — What effect would a compromised site have on the organization?
Recognizability — Do adversaries easily recognize a site or asset to be valuable?

A Military Example

TARGET	C	A	R	V	E	R	OVERALL RANK
COMMAND POST	5	2	5	3	4	5	24
FEEDING POINT	4	3	3	3	3	2	18
MILITARY CAMP	3	4	1	3	2	5	18
STAGING AREA	2	5	1	5	2	5	20
WEAPONS CACHE	4	5	3	2	2	1	17

A Business Example

DEPART-MENT	C	A	R	V	E	R	OVERALL RANK
FINANCE	4	3	3	3	3	2	18
HR	4	5	3	2	2	1	17
OPERA-TIONS	3	4	1	3	2	5	18
PURCHAS-ING	2	5	1	5	2	5	20
QUALITY	5	2	5	3	4	5	24

The CARVER Technique

The CARVER Technique is widely used in military, law enforcement, and security settings to evaluate targets in order to best allocate resources for potential attacks. It's a defense-oriented process designed to predict and defend against hostile actions. "CARVER" stands for:

Criticality—the Importance of the Target

How essential is this object or operation to success?

Accessibility—the Ease of Entry

How free is access to unauthorized persons?

Recuperability—Time to Recover

How easy would it be to replace the function of this or that?

Vulnerability—Internal Weaknesses or Flaws

What defects or limitations could be exploited by outsiders?

Effect—Impact of Target's Loss

What effects would follow the removal of this facility?

Recognizability—Desirability as a Target

How easily can a competitor see the value of this target?

Things to Remember

CARVER is also used by the competition to select potential targets and guide offense-destruction strategies. Another reason to gather intelligence about the competition—if you know them, you're better able to predict their goals and plans.

> Nothing is foolproof because fools are so damn clever.
>
> —Modern Proverb

Nothing can be perfectly secure because of the costs and inconveniences that level of security would create, plus the fact that competitors are always devising new strategies to make honest people's lives more difficult. Therefore, priorities must be set. The Technique sets priorities as objectively as possible.

CARVER analyses are most accurate and effective when they involve stakeholders from across the organization. Advice from outside experts can also be valuable, adding another level of objectivity.

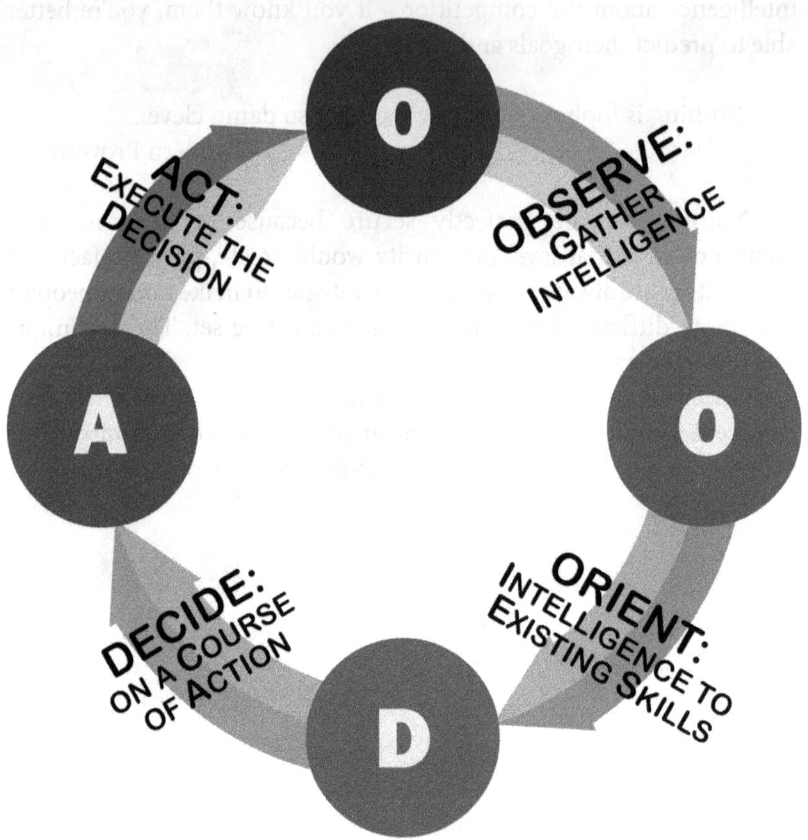

POSITIVES:

- **Leadership must devolve to lower levels.**
- **Provides real flexibility in real time.**
- **Can deal with multiple situations simultaneously.**
- **Quick actions make countermeasures difficult.**

NEGATIVES:

- **Operates only on a tactical level.**
- **Cannot act when permissions are required.**
- **Can be overwhelmed by evolving situations.**
- **Requires top-tier situational awareness.**

The OODA Loop

It's called the Loop to emphasize the continuous nature of decision-making in dynamic, competitive environments. Its power lies in its simplicity and flexibility.

Method:

1. Observe

Crisis managers continuously watch for changes in their situation.

2. Orient

Analyze what you see based on everything you know.

3. Decide

Formulate a best-guess course of action.

4. Act

Execute your decision without delay.

Remember:

- It allows you maximum flexibility in fast-changing scenarios.
- It allows you to deal with multiple unrelated problems that arise simultaneously.
- It operates entirely on tactics. Some say that winning is the sum total of all the tactical actions. Tactics, however, don't add up to a strategy.
- It cannot act when permissions are required unless real-time communications are certain.
- It can be overwhelmed by evolving situations.
- Demands top-tier situational awareness by on-site crisis managers.

The Attack Tree Analysis

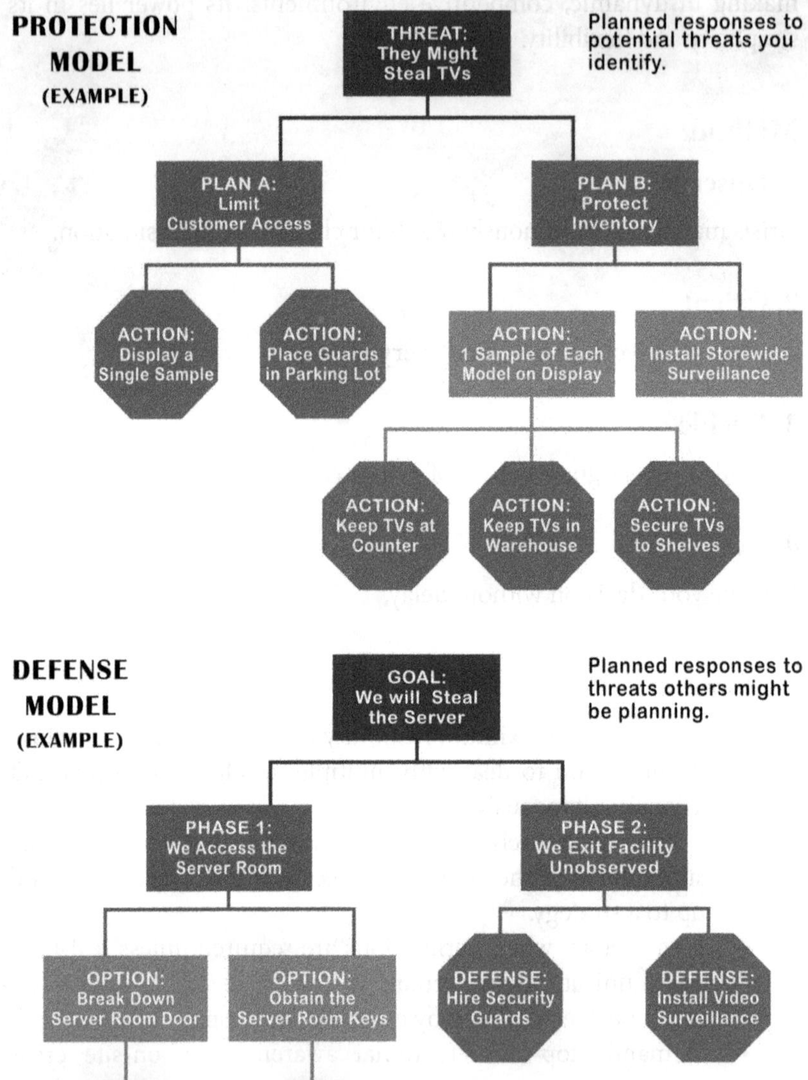
PROTECTION
MODEL
(EXAMPLE)
THREAT: They Might Steal TVs
Planned responses to potential threats you identify.
PLAN A: Limit Customer Access
PLAN B: Protect Inventory
ACTION: Display a Single Sample
ACTION: Place Guards in Parking Lot
ACTION: 1 Sample of Each Model on Display
ACTION: Install Storewide Surveillance
ACTION: Keep TVs at Counter
ACTION: Keep TVs in Warehouse
ACTION: Secure TVs to Shelves
DEFENSE
MODEL
(EXAMPLE)
GOAL: We will Steal the Server
Planned responses to threats others might be planning.
PHASE 1: We Access the Server Room
PHASE 2: We Exit Facility Unobserved
OPTION: Break Down Server Room Door
OPTION: Obtain the Server Room Keys
DEFENSE: Hire Security Guards
DEFENSE: Install Video Surveillance
ACTION: Install a Security Door
ACTION: Install an Electronic Lock

The Attack Tree Analysis (ATA)

The Perspective

This Analysis can provide additional insights into vulnerabilities and assist in countermeasures development by breaking down potential attack scenarios into manageable components.

ATA takes a top-down approach. It starts by identifying end results and working back to preventative or curative APs. This visual representation provides a comprehensive overview of potential vulnerabilities, attack vectors, and countermeasures.

Components

Root Node

Blue in the above examples—represents the main objective of an attacker, such as extracting sensitive information. It serves as the starting point for the analysis and branches out into various attack paths.

Attack Paths

Green—the ways an attacker can achieve their objective, broken down into sub-goals or steps.

Leaf Nodes

Orange—the lowest-level attack steps or vulnerabilities, including specific actions an attacker might take.

Countermeasures

Red—defenses that mitigate the risks. Specific countermeasures are assigned to specific nodes in the tree to clarify the effectiveness of existing security measures or identify gaps needing to be addressed.

Requirements

1. Comprehensive Risk Assessment, a structured approach to understanding potential attack vectors and vulnerabilities and assisting in developing comprehensive assessment and mitigation efforts.
2. Proactive Defense Planning enables organizations to proactively defend by visualizing attack paths, identifying weak points, and preparing defense alternatives.
3. Resource Allocation Optimization through the identification of critical areas.
4. Compliance with regulatory requirements goes more smoothly when thorough risk assessments have been completed and appropriate countermeasures are in place.

Emerging Threats

Some threats are envisioned but not yet fully understood or realized—rapid changes in modern technology have created opportunities for you and your competition. An ATA can identify potential targets based on past experiences.

Remember

- Technology, for all its amazing capabilities, has limitations.
- Humans, for all our amazing capabilities, have limitations.
- The as-yet-unrealized full potential of artificial intelligence (AI) must be combined with basic human skills—the legendary "Mark-1 Eyeball" to maximize the effectiveness of both.

THE EISENHOWER MATRIX

THE ORIGINAL

	URGENT	NOT URGENT
IMPORTANT	**1:** Do These First **Time Critical:** Overdue or Due Now **Value:** Adds to Short-term Goals **Your Attention:** Required	**2:** Do These Soon **Time Sensitive:** Due Soon or Later **Value:** Adds to Long-Term Goals **Your Attention:** Required
NOT IMPORTANT	**3:** Delegate These **Time:** Overdue or Due Now **Value:** Adds Some **Your Attention:** Useful	**4:** Do These When Convenient **Not Time Sensitive:** Due Whenever **Value:** Adds Little **Your Attention:** Not Required

THE Jochen Matrix (Sample) (Eisenhower Expanded)

		URGENCY				
		TODAY (5)	THIS WEEK (4)	THIS MONTH (3)	THIS QUARTER (2)	BELOW MY PAY GRADE (1)
IMPORTANCE	I DO IT (4)	20	16	12	8	4
	I OVERSEE IT (3)	15	12	9	6	3
	I DELEGATE IT (2)	10	8	6	4	2
	BELOW MY PAY GRADE (1)	5	4	3	2	1

The Eisenhower Matrix

The Management Question

When a path to success—COA & AP—has been laid out, how do crisis managers most efficiently and effectively manage a crisis?

They divide the tasks and assign them to the personnel best suited to deal with them.

Importance versus Urgency

"Importance" prioritizes the actions that end the crisis.

"Urgency" prioritizes the actions that safeguard people, then equipment, then business.

Who needs to complete which actions?

The crisis manager (owner or executive) ***needs*** to do certain things.

What they don't ***need*** to do or ***can't*** do ***needs*** to be delegated to assistants or technical experts.

Which actions have no priority within the crisis?

What doesn't ***need*** to be done to solve the crisis ***needs*** to be set aside until later.

The Matrix Expanded

The original Matrix is a paired absolute: Things are either urgent or they are not. Things are either important or they are not. Real life is seldom black and white; there are shades of gray. The Matrix can be expanded to several levels using a CARVER analysis or other tools to set priorities.

Crisis Response Levels

Instinctive Responses — Short-Term

At times, acting quickly is the highest priority, for example: Where there's a clear and present danger of damage or injury, where criminal activity is detected, when natural or human-caused disasters strike, and when actions by a stakeholder change the core nature of a situation.

Incidents that require immediate responses are, happily, exceedingly rare.

Tactical Responses — Mid-Term

A crisis management team is organized. Statutes might require government agencies to be notified. Engineering starts asking the "5 Whys." Other departments deal with costs, legalities, public relations, and other consequences.

Strategic Responses — Long-term — Recovery & Prevention Plans

The crisis management team determines long-term recovery through prevention planning. Repeating that old sage, "It costs you nothing to correct a mistake that never gets made."

Remember

Crises have costs—money, time, materials, people. You can't make money in a crisis; your goal is to minimize your losses.

Your company's most valuable resource is your people. Corporate culture is key—your people will walk thr!ough fire for you if (and only if) they know you're walking the fire ahead of them.

About the Author

Jochen Schwenk

CEO of Crisis Control Solutions LLC, based in Naples, Florida, and Schwenk AG, headquartered in Zurich, Switzerland, Jochen Schwenk is a trailblazer in risk mitigation and crisis management. Widely regarded as a leading authority in his field, Jochen's expertise is sought after by governments, industries, and Fortune 500 companies.

A distinguished author and founding member of Harvard's Presidents Circle, Jochen is also a member of other prestigious organizations, including the Forbes Council and Harvard Square. His deep understanding of complex challenges stems from an extensive background in military and intelligence operations—details of which remain deliberately discreet—adding a unique edge to his approach to risk and crisis management.

Together with his team of passionate and highly skilled professionals, Jochen has developed industry-defining strategies, particularly in addressing critical supply chain issues that impact global markets. His firm's services span a wide spectrum, from geopolitical consulting to proactive solutions for industrial disruptions, always staying ahead of the curve to deliver unparalleled value to clients.

Under Jochen's visionary leadership, Crisis Control Solutions and Schwenk AG have set the gold standard in crisis preparedness and resolution, empowering organizations to face the unthinkable with confidence and resilience.